Michael M. Dediu

It is getting truer and truer
- we urgently need the
World Constitution

Moving from anarchic changes, to
balanced transition to the
Constitution of the World

DERC Publishing House
Nashua, New Hampshire, U. S. A.

Published and printed in the
United States of America
On the Great Seal of the United States are included:
E Pluribus Unum (Out of many, one)
Annuit Coeptis (He has approved of the undertakings)
Novus Ordo Seclorum (New order of the ages)

Library of Congress Control Number: 2020912275
Dediu, Michael M.

Truer and truer – we urgently need the World Constitution
Moving from anarchic changes, to balanced transition to the
Constitution of the World

ISBN-13: 978-1-950999-17-0

MSG0399696_61Ju0XM9Ishu7Oc4yJ9m
MSG0399799_RaMsT6607e8oe57k9f0c
1-9006453921
26PDBCGO
1-44Y7KD3

Preface

Every single second clearly shows that the thousands of years old habits of using wars and violence, to change something in the world, are still in use, therefore all people want to have a much better, peaceful and harmonious new Constitution of the World, just published on 7 March 2020.

It is truer and truer every moment that the big family of over 7.7 billions of people living on Earth want a good and friendly implementation of this new, sharp, clear, nonviolent and sustainable Constitution of the World, which will finally eliminate wars, nuclear arms, and many other deadly habits of the past.

Churchill, over 60 years ago, said astoundingly correct that "If the human race wishes to have a prolonged and indefinite period of material prosperity, they have only got to behave in a peaceful and helpful way toward one another". This fits perfectly with having this new lovely Constitution, which will start the next 10,000 years of harmony.

In this book we present new ideas regarding this pleasant implementation of the new Constitution of the World, which, finally, will create the conditions for a pacific, free and prosperous new country, Peaceful Terra.

Michael M. Dediu, Ph. D.

Nashua, New Hampshire, U. S. A., 8 July 2020

USA: Chicago, 1837: London Guarantee Bldg. (1923, 22 fl, 96 m), on North Michigan Avenue.

Table of Contents

DM21. Nice one thousand districts 33

DM22. Free navigation everywhere 34

DM23. Certainly no borders 35

DM24. Fast first implementation..36

DM25. Just four levels of world management 37

  DM25.1. Level 1 Management 38

  DM25.2. Level 2 Management 39

    From Paris to Abuja..40

    From Zürich to N'Djamena..42

    From Zagreb to Kananga 43

    From Athens to Bujumbura 44

    From Kiev to Nairobi 45

    From Addis Ababa to Yerevan 46

    From Riyadh to Muscat 47

    From Chelyabinsk to Malé 48

    From Bishkek to Nagpur 49

    From Chennai to Tomsk...50

    From Kathmandu to Abakan..51

    From Dibrugarh to Chiang Mai 52

    From Bangkok to Ulan Bator...53

    From Cirebon to Hong Kong 54

    From Nanchang to Kupang 55

    From Pyongyang to Melbourne 56

    From Anchorage to Hermosillo..57

    From Regina to Lima 58

Japan: Tokyo Metropolitan Government Building, 243 m, 48 floors, 1991, in Shinjuku, with two observation decks on floor 45, 202 m.

DM1. Purposes

SUN: A good Constitution of the World needs a clear method to implement it consistently and efficiently – do you have such a method?

EARTH: Yes, we do – Dediu Method, which contains many easy, clear and friendly ideas.

SUN: This is great – Dediu also created the Constitution of the World, therefore one can expect a Dediu Method to nicely implement the Constitution.

EARTH: Yes, this method is peaceful, calm, friendly and results oriented, for people's benefit.

SUN: Good – let's see what ideas it contains.

EARTH: The central idea of Dediu Method is to completely eliminate war and any type of conflicts.

SUN: Well, excellent idea – and how the method will implement it?

EARTH: Using all the positive examples from the past, when some good people tried to do some reductions of armaments, and they actually had some success – the method says that we will build on this, and will do much better. We will start with small meetings between the major military powers, to immediately begin the elimination of all nuclear arms. Then, step by step, all the countries will begin to eliminate all war-related equipment.

SUN: The method has a good start for a peaceful and harmonious world.

EARTH: Yes, Dediu Method is based on the fact that people want peace and harmony, and they will have exactly what they want – nobody can stop this process.

SUN: Certainly!

EARTH: After eliminating all arms, naturally the people will move to consolidate a peaceful and harmonious world by implementing the new Constitution, using the handy method.

France, L'Opéra de Paris (or L'Académie Nationale de Musique, or l'Opéra Garnier, or Le Palais Garnier, or L'Opéra), a 1,979-seat opera house, built from 1861 to 1875, now mainly used for ballet.

DM2. Freedom, good families and prosperity

SUN: What are examples of important ideas used by the method?

EARTH: Freedom, dignity, good families, prosperity and respect are examples of basic concepts in the method, and they are essential for rapidly implementing the new Constitution.

Italy, Rome: The steps (cordonata) to the Piazza del Campidoglio, which was built around 1050 and updated by Michelangelo around 1535.

DM3. Health first

SUN: What about good health and good education?

EARTH: They are sine qua non requirements for all people, and the method certainly uses them constantly. The coronavirus pandemic is one more example why the new Constitution needs to be quickly implemented using the method, which has a clear description of the many medical improvements that are needed.

Chicago, 1837: Wrigley Bldg. (1922, 30 fl, 133 m center-right), River Plaza (1977, 56 fl, 160 m, center-left), North Bridge – Plaza 440 (1991, 49 fl, 146 m, next left).

DM4. Responsive atmosphere

SUN: Does the method include friendly atmosphere?

EARTH: Certainly, and we will not stop until this dream becomes a reality, and the new Constitution is unquestionably the necessary tool to arrive there quickly.

The method shows that the move to a much better one country on Earth is not a sprint - it is a long, steady and pleasant marathon. Burnout may come for some leaders, because isn't just about keeping a ship afloat, but it's about not always having full control. Studies have shown that the loss of control is a big stressor. To work the longest hours and to bear the greatest burden is not so effective. Having clear priorities and reserving energy are important. Recommendations for the new leaders include: delegate, walk. outside, in the Sun, for half an hour or more. Sleep at least 7 hours/night, also meditate in a positive way, and show gratitude. Narcissistic leaders are not good, avoid logistics chaos, collaborate with NGOs and local governments in new ways, and always be a people-focused leader.

DM5. Need of World Government

SUN: Goethe said something important, over 190 years ago.

EARTH: Yes: "Which government is the best? The one that teaches us to govern ourselves." We want to reach this with our Friendly World Government, in which case the sustainability of peace, freedom and prosperity will be guaranteed for long time.

SUN: What about the World Government?

EARTH: Dediu method is clear: World Government must have the safety and wellbeing of all the people in the world as the highest priority. All people agree with this idea – there must be a constant effort to implement this idea, using the new Constitution.

Italy, Roma: Detail from the left side of the fountain in front of the staircase of Palazzo Senatorio, showing the river god of the Tiber.

DM6. History of peaceful-oriented results

SUN: I remember, my dear Earth, not too long ago, about 66 M of years, there were just a few people on you, then, about 10,000 years ago (8000 BC), there were around 1 million of people, and they had plenty of conflicts and primitive wars.

EARTH: Yes, my good Sun, now I have a great family of over 7.74 B, but they still have plenty of conflicts and not-so-primitive wars.

SUN: Are they happy with this?

EARTH: Not at all – now they want at least 10,000 years to live in one peaceful, free and prosperous country, let's call it Peaceful Terra!

SUN: Is the method looking to history?

EARTH: Certainly, the method considers the last several thousands of years, when people accumulated a big amount of peaceful-oriented results, experience and knowledge, and we need to use all this good amount of peaceful-oriented results, experience and knowledge, for a much better future, and the new Constitution will give us all the necessary structure to achieve this objective.

DM7. Density

SUN: Having a total area of over 509 M km^2, and land area over 148 M km^2 is pretty nice for a country.

EARTH: Well, you cannot ask for more, it is about 2 ha of land for each person, or about 52 people/ km^2 - and in the future we'll expand to the Moon, asteroids, Mars, etc.

France, Paris: Galeries Lafayette (1895, left) on Blvd Haussmann (left) and Sephora store (center) near Rue de la Chaussée-d'Antin (right).

DM8. Common-sense rules

SUN: What does the Dediu Method say about rules?

EARTH: Very clear and sharp: no more than 2,000 rules, on maximum 1,000 pages, period! You see, from a hyperinflation of bureaucratic rules and regulations, the method we'll take us to several short common-sense rules, in less than 5 months.

Italy, Roma: Palazzo Senatorio (back, now Rome's city hall), built around 1250-1350 atop the Tabularium (78 BC), and the equestrian statue of Marcus Aurelius (121 – 180, Roman Emperor 161 – 180).

DM9. Just ten regions

SUN: What is the fundamental idea of the Dediu Method about the regions?

EARTH: Yes, this fundamental idea of the method is to have just 10 simple and friendly regions of around 770 M people each, because it is really helpful for better administration of the planet. The implementation of this idea will require intense and friendly work of many people, with the help of the United Nations, and the results will be astonishing and much celebrated.

Japan, Kyoto (678): a traditional gate, similar to the Karamon gate (1573, for the Nishi Hongan-ji Temple ("Western Temple of the Original Vow", 1602, on the west side of Horikawa Dori).

DM10. Bern, Libreville (Gabon) and Oxford (UK)

SUN: What other important ideas are in the method regarding these 10 regions?

EARTH: One first idea is to call the Regions with only two characters, for simpler computer processing: R0, R1,…,R9.

A second fundamental idea is to use meridians for the delimitation of the regions, thus having a simple, impartial, friendly and practical technique, very easy to implement.

The third idea is to start defining the first region R0: from meridian 0 to 15^0 E.

The fourth idea is to have two capitals – one in the northern hemisphere, and the other one in the southern hemisphere – for the region R0 the method chose Bern (Switzerland) and Libreville (Gabon).

The fifth idea is to use the assistance from a third city from another region, for homogeneity and high-quality management – for R0 the method chose Oxford (UK). This first Region R0 has parts of western Europe and central-western Africa.

Japan, Kyoto (678): the railway station (the second-largest station building (after Nagoya), 15 floors, 70 m high, 470 m wide, 238,000 m^2 floor area 1877, 1928, 1997). Shopping mall, hotel.

DM11. Warsaw, Pretoria (South Africa), Miami (USA)

SUN: What does the method suggest for the region R1?

EARTH: R1 will be between meridians 15^0 E and 30^0 E, with capitals at Warsaw (Poland), and Pretoria (South Africa), and assistance from Miami (FL, USA). The distance between Warsaw (Poland) and Pretoria (South Africa) is over 8,800 km, and from Pretoria to Miami is about 13,000 km – it gives a good world perspective.

Italy, Roma: Forum Romanum (80 BC, right), Temple of Saturn 42 BC, center, Arch of Severus 203, center-left, Temple of Vespasian 80, left.

DM12. Moscow, Cairo (Egypt), Grenoble (France)

SUN: Now let's see the region R2.

EARTH: Yes, R2 is between 30^0 E and 45^0 E and has capitals in Moscow (Russia) and Cairo (Egypt), with friendly assistance from Grenoble (France) -they look close to an equilateral geodesic triangle, because Moscow to Cairo is over 2,800 km, from Cairo to Grenoble over 2,700 km, and from Grenoble to Moscow over 2,500 km.

France, Bourse de Paris in Palais Brongniart (1808 – 1826, by Napoleon), seen through Rue de la Bourse, from Rue de Richelieu.

DM13.   Nur-Sultan   (Kazakhstan),   Karachi, Montpellier

SUN: Now we arrived at the interesting recommendation for the Region R3.

EARTH: Yes, the method recommends to be between the meridians 45^0 E and 75^0 E, with its first capitals at Nur-Sultan (former Astana, Kazakhstan) and Karachi (Pakistan), the kind assistance coming from Montpellier (France). Nur-Sultan (or Astana, Kazakhstan) to Karachi (Pakistan) is about 3,000 km, and Karachi to Montpellier (France) is about 6,000 km.

USA: Chicago, 1837: from the Skydeck (floor 103, 412 m) of Willis Tower (1973, 108 floors, 527 m) a view of the south part of Chicago, with the South Branch of Chicago River (center) and Lake Michigan (left).

DM14. New Delhi, Novosibirsk, Magdeburg (Germany)

SUN: Dediu Method gives us this nice region R4.

EARTH: Yes, between 75^0 E and 85^0 E, with capitals at New Delhi (India) and Novosibirsk (Russia), collaborating with Magdeburg (Germany). We notice that New Delhi (India) to Novosibirsk (Russia) is about 3,000 km, and New Delhi to Magdeburg (Germany) is about 5,900 km.

Italy, Roma: The Arch of Septimius Severus (145 – 211, Emperor 193 - 211), built in 203 to commemorate the victory over the Parthians in 197.

DM15. Krasnoyarsk, Ürümqi (China), Avignon

SUN: Now comes the attractive region R5.

EARTH: Yes, between 85^0 E and 100^0 E, with its first capitals at Krasnoyarsk (Russia) and Ürümqi (China), working with Avignon (France). Krasnoyarsk (Russia) to Ürümqi (China) is about 1,400 km, and Ürümqi to Avignon (France) is over 6,300 km.

France, Paris: Basilique du Sacré-Cœur (1875 – 1914, 83 m), located at the summit of the butte Montmartre, the highest point in the city.

DM16. Jakarta (Indonesia), Beijing (China), Neuchâtel

SUN: Can't wait for the region R6…

EARTH: Yes, between 100^0 E - 115^0 E, with capitals in Jakarta (Indonesia) and Beijing (China), and friendly assistance from Neuchâtel (Switzerland) - it is really inspiring. Jakarta (Indonesia) to Beijing (China) is over 5,200 km, and Neuchâtel (Switzerland) to Beijing is over 8,000 km.

Italy, Rome (753 BC): Sapienza – Università di Roma (1303). The Chapel with the inscription "Omnium Artifex Sapientia, Pius XII P.M., 1948".

DM17. Tokyo, Sydney (Australia), Malmö (Sweden)

SUN: And now the nice region R7.

EARTH: Yes, from 115^0 E to 180^0 and has capitals in Tokyo (Japan) and Sydney (Australia), with kind help from Malmö (Sweden). Tokyo (Japan) to Sydney (Australia) is over 7,800 km, and Sydney to Malmö (Sweden) is over 16,000 km.

Japan: Inzai Post Office, 300 m north-est from the entrance to the Inzai (Chiba) campus of Tokyo Denki University (TDU, founded in 1907) in Muzai-Gakuendai, 34 km north-east of Tokyo.

DM18. Washington, Mexico City, Bellinzona (Switzerland)

SUN: Tell me about this lovely region R8.

EARTH: Sure, R8 is between 180^0 and 70^0 W and has capitals in Washington (USA) and Mexico City (Mexico), with inspiring help from Bellinzona (Switzerland). Washington (USA) to Mexico City (Mexico) is over 3,000 km, and Mexico City to Bellinzona (Switzerland) is about 9,600 km.

Forum Romanum (80 BC, right), Temple of Saturn 42 BC, center, Arch of Severus 203, center-left, Temple of Vespasian 80, left

DM19.   Halifax   (Canada),   Brasilia,   Biel (Switzerland)

SUN: Nice idea with this fascinating 10th region R9.

EARTH: Yes, indeed, from 70^0 W to meridian 0, has capitals in Halifax (Canada) and Brasilia (Brazil), with friendly assistance from Biel (Switzerland). We note that Halifax (Canada) to Brasilia (Brazil) is over 6,900 km, and from Brasilia to Biel (Switzerland) is over 8,800 Km.

Paris: Gare de l'Est (1849, 30 platforms for Strasbourg, Mulhouse, Venice Simplon Orient Express), in Place du 11 Novembre 1918.

DM20. Great one hundred sub-regions

SUN: Here is another good idea in Dediu Method - each of the 10 regions will be divided by meridians in 10 sub-regions S00,...., S99, each with about 77 M people, and this will certainly require some work.

EARTH: No question – but local competent administrators, with some help from the capitals and others, will find good practical delimitations between very friendly sub-regions, each with about 77 M people. The delimitations will be flexible, in order to maintain a relatively constant 77 M people.

Japan, Kyoto (678): traditional houses near the Nishi Hongan-ji Temple ("Western Temple of the Original Vow", 1602).

DM21. Nice one thousand districts

SUN: Nice idea about the 100 sub-regions to be divided in 10 districts.

EARTH: Indeed, the districts D000, D001,..., D999, each with about 7.7 M people, and the local details become more important. Each of the districts will have their current small and big cities. Detailed work will be necessary at local level, with help from outside, but everybody is interested in better life and harmony. Another good idea from Dediu Method: having telework, many people will have a northern residence and a southern residence, seasonally moving from one to the other, to avoid extreme cold or heat, and having the same hour.

Temple of Saturn 42 BC, right, Arch of Severus 203, center-right, Temple of Vespasian 80 center, east side of Palazzo Senatorio, left.

DM22. Free navigation everywhere

SUN: Another important idea from the method: all the oceans will belong to all the regions, therefore will be managed and maintained by those regions, to be free of any piracy or other bad activity.

EARTH: Sure, and the World Police will help when necessary. Look at this idea: free navigation and free use of the oceans will be guaranteed for all people.

Paris: Atelier Brancusi (Constantin Brancusi, sculptor, 1876 – 1957), Musée national d'art moderne, left of the Centre Georges Pompidou (1971–1977 in the Beaubourg area), on Rue Rambuteau.

DM23. Certainly no borders

SUN: This is a great idea from the method: after waiting many thousands of years, my Peaceful Terra will have no borders.

EARTH: Yes, indeed, there will be just simple administrative delimitations, and all these delimitations between regions, as well as between sub-regions, will be flexible – they will be changed after each census (5 years), for maintaining a balanced number of people in all regions (around 770 M), and sub-regions (around 77 M).

SUN: Our author has a nice aphorism...

EARTH: Yes, "In order to gain wisdom, and therefore to be closer to happiness, "vitam mutaveris saepe in meliores actus" (change your life often for the better)". Everything changes, therefore we all have to change in better too – from Latin: Omnia mutantur nos et mutamur in illis. Also, Darwin (circa 140 years ago): "It is not the strongest of the species that survive, nor the most intelligent, but the one most responsive to change".

DM24. Fast first implementation

SUN: Tell me about the idea on the administrative delimitations.

EARTH: The administrative delimitations will be moved a few kilometers east or west, to reach a balanced population. Because all the people are in the same country, it is normal to modify a little its regions, for better administration, to make everybody happy.

Italy, Roma: On Ponte Palatino (1891), Pons Cestius (46 BC, left), Isola Tiberina (center), Basilica San Bartolomeo all'Isola (990, center).

DM25. Just four levels of world management

SUN: Now let's talk about the method's great ideas on Government of my Peaceful Terra.

EARTH: Sure - the family of over 7. 7 B people on Peaceful Terra will have four levels of world management; however, at the local level, if needed, it could be one or two more levels of local managers (mayors, town managers, county managers – let me repeat: all levels of management must be friendly, helpful, fast, polite, modest and smart).

Paris, Montmartre, Boulevard de Rochechouart (600 m south of Basilique du Sacré-Cœur (1914)): buildings near Anvers Metro Station and stores like Sympa.

DM25.1. Level 1 Management

SUN: From Dediu Method you have Level 1 Management, with 1,000 L1 friendly managers.

EARTH: Yes, I am proud of these devoted 1,000 L1 friendly managers for the 1,000 districts on Earth. They will supervise and assist the mayors and town managers from their district, for a total of about 7,700,000 people in each district. Each of the 1,000 L1 friendly managers will be located in a central city from their districts – some could be the mayors of those cities, but with new responsibilities for the whole district.

USA: Chicago, 1837: from the Skydeck (floor 103, 412 m) of Willis Tower (1973, 108 floors, 527 m) a view of the north-east part of Chicago, with Chase Tower (1969, 60 fl, 260 m, center-right down), and Lake Michigan (up).

DM25.2. Level 2 Management

SUN: What about the Level 2 Management, with 100 L2 friendly managers?

EARTH: All 100 L2 friendly managers for the 100 sub-regions will supervise and assist the 10 L1 managers of the 10 districts of each sub-region, for a total of about 77,000,000 people for each sub-region. Let's remember this idea from the method: these 100 L2 friendly managers will move each month between the two capitals of each of the 100 sub-regions.

Italy, Roma: The Basilica Santa Maria in Cosmedin (1085) with the Bocca della Verità (Mouth of Truth) in its porch.

From Paris to Abuja

SUN: From Dediu Method let's see the first 5 sub-regions of R0.

EARTH: - The sub-region R00 will have the capitals Paris (France) and Niamey (Niger) – assistance from Magdeburg (Germany).
- The sub-region R01 will have the capitals Brussels (Belgium) and Porto-Novo (Benin) - assistance from Toronto (Canada).
- The sub-region R02 will have the capitals Amsterdam (Netherlands) and Algiers (Algeria) - assistance from Graz (Austria).
- The sub-region R03 will have the capitals Luxembourg (Luxembourg) and Sao Tome (Sao Tome and Principe) - assistance from Adelaide (Australia).
- The sub-region R04 will have the capitals of Abuja (Nigeria) and Bochum (Germany) - assistance from Nikko (Japan).

The practical implementation of all these sub-regions is really easy – for example, for R00, the mayor from the assistance city Magdeburg (Germany) sends kind e-mails to the mayors of Paris and Niamery, inviting them to start the discussions, and to propose the initial delimitations of R00, within 3 days. Then friendly discussions about the details will also include the neighboring sub-regions R01 and R99, and within 3 days they will decide the delimitations of R00, which will not be perfect, but good enough to start the delightful process of building the sub-regions of a brand new and much better single country. Then they will immediately start to work to improve the living standards of all their people, by establishing a list of priorities. Weekly and monthly reviews will help to improve their initial plans, and work will continue in an atmosphere of collaboration and friendship. When difficulties appear, assistance will be requested from medical and other assistants, as well as from the upper management. No conflicts of any nature are acceptable. As in any big family, all will work in peace and harmony, for the benefit of all people.

France, Paris: A copy (made in 1964) of the sculpture "The Dance" (1868 – 1869, 4.2 m by 3 m, with a highly animated central male dancer, surrounded by six dancing women (the original is now in the Musée d'Orsay)) by Jean-Baptiste Carpeaux (1827 – 1875, he closely studied the sculpture of Michelangelo (1475 – 1564) in Rome; Garnier commissioned Carpeaux in 1865), on the left side of the right outer bay on the façade of l'Opéra de Paris (1875).

From Zürich to N'Djamena

SUN: Also, from Dediu Method, let's see now the next 5 sub-regions.

EARTH: - The sub-region R05 will have the capitals Malabo (Equatorial Guinea), Zürich (Switzerland) - assistance from Leeds (UK).
- The sub-region R06 will have the capitals Oslo (Norway) and Tunis (Tunisia) - assistance from Sheffield (UK).
- The sub-region R07 will have the capitals Roma (Italy) and Luanda (Angola) - assistance from Yamagata (Japan).
- The sub-region R08 will have the capitals in Berlin (Germany) and Tripoli (Libya) - assistance from New York (USA).
- The sub-region R09 will have the capitals Prague (Czech Republic) and N'Djamena (Chad) - assistance from Brisbane (Australia).

Japan, Kyoto (678): typical small streets near the Nishi Hongan-ji Temple ("Western Temple of the Original Vow", 1602).

From Zagreb to Kananga

SUN: Moving now to region R1 its first great 5 sub-regions.

EARTH: - The sub-region R10 will have the capitals in Zagreb (Croatia) and Brazzaville (Congo) - assistance from Nantes (France).
- The sub-region R11 will have the capitals in Vienna (Austria), Windhoek (Namibia) - assistance from Bilbao (Spain).
- The sub-region R12 will have the capitals in Stockholm (Sweden), Bangui (Central African Republic) - assistance from Florence (Italy).
- The sub-region R13 will have the capitals in Budapest (Hungary), Rundu (Namibia) - assistance from Monaco (Monaco).
- The sub-region R14 will have the capitals in Belgrade (Serbia), Kananga (Democratic Republic of Congo) - assistance from Liverpool (UK).

Italy, Roma: La Bocca della Verità (50 AD) is a sculpture carved from Pavonazzo marble, with a man-like face (Oceanus).

From Athens to Bujumbura

SUN: The next 5 sub-regions are really interesting.

EARTH: Yes, - The sub-region R15 will have the capitals in Athens (Greece), Mongu (Zambia) - assistance from Los Angeles (CA, USA).
- The sub-region R16 will have the capitals in Helsinki (Finland) and Gaborone (Botswana) - assistance from Montreal (Canada).
- The sub-region R17 will have the capitals in Bucharest (Romania) and Gaborone (Botswana) - assistance from Philadelphia (PA, USA).
- The sub-region R18 will have the capitals in Minsk (Belarus) and Maseru (Lesotho) - assistance from Orleans (France).
- The sub-region R19 will have the capitals in Chisinau (Republic of Moldova) and Bujumbura (Burundi) - assistance from Hamburg (Germany).

USA: Chicago, 1837: from the Skydeck (floor 103, 412 m) of Willis Tower (1973, 108 floors, 527 m) a view of the east part of Chicago, with Chase Tower (1969, 60 fl, 260 m, left down), Maurice Rothschild Bldg. (1928, 62 m, center) and Lake Michigan.

From Kiev to Nairobi

SUN: The region R2 now – first 5 subregions.

EARTH: - The sub-region R20 will have the capitals in Kiev (Ukraine) and Kigali (Rwanda) - assistance from Ottawa (Canada).
- The sub-region R21 will have the capitals in Ankara (Turkey) and Khartoum (Sudan) - assistance from Salzburg (Austria).
- The sub-region R22 will have the capitals in Lilongwe (Malawi) and Nicosia (Cyprus) - assistance from Dallas (TX, USA).
- The sub-region R23 will have the capitals in Jerusalem (Israel) and Dodoma (Tanzania) - assistance from Strasbourg (France).
- The sub-region R24 will have the capitals in Damascus (Syria) and Nairobi (Kenya) - assistance from Stuttgart (Germany).

Italy, Roma: The Circus Maximus (550 BC – 549 AD), the world largest stadium (250,000 people) for chariot races, for over 1,000 years.

From Addis Ababa to Yerevan

SUN: I cannot wait to see the next 5 regions from the method.

EARTH: - The sub-region R25 will have the capitals in Krasnodar (Russia) and Addis Ababa (Ethiopia) - assistance from Marseille (France).
- The sub-region R26 will have the capitals in Rostov-on-Don (Russia) and Asmara (Eritrea) - assistance from Leipzig (Germany).
- The sub-region R27 will have the capitals in Stavropol (Russia) and Djibouti (Djibouti) - assistance from Zürich (Switzerland).
- The sub-region R28 will have the capitals in Mosul (Iraq) and Moroni (Comoros) - assistance from Linz (Austria).
- The sub-region R29 will have the capitals in Yerevan (Armenia) and Baghdad (Iraq) - assistance from Göttingen (Germany).

Paris, Île de la Cité, Pont au Change (1860): La Conciergerie (Palace of French Kings (950 – 1358), on Quai de l'Horloge, left), Pont Neuf (1578-1607, center, at the west corner of Île de la Cité).

From Riyadh to Muscat

SUN: Obviously, region R3 surprises with its first 5 sub-regions.

EARTH: - The sub-region R30 will have the capitals in Riyadh (Saudi Arabia) and Mogadishu (Somalia) - assistance from Bonn (Germany).
- The sub-region R31 will have the capitals in Baku (Azerbaijan) and Antananarivo (Madagascar) - assistance from Le Mans (France).
- The sub-region R32 will have the capitals in Oral (Kazakhstan) and Tehran (Iran) - assistance from Pisa (Italy).
- The sub-region R33 will have the capitals in Ashgabat (Turkmenistan) and Abu Dhabi (United Arab Emirates) - assistance from Wolfsburg (Germany).
- The sub-region R34 will have the capitals in Magnitogorsk (Russia) and Muscat (Oman) - assistance from Toulouse (France).

Japan, Kyoto (678): the gate (left) to Shinshu Honbyo Temple (1321, called until 1987 Higashi Hongan-Ji, with a nice Shosei Garden, open 5:50 AM to 5:30 PM), on the west side of Karasuma Dori, north of Shichijo Dori and south of Hanayacho Dori.

From Chelyabinsk to Malé

SUN: No question that the next 5 sub-regions are fascinating.

EARTH: - The sub-region R35 will have the capitals in Chelyabinsk (Russia) and Herat (Afghanistan) - assistance from Basel (Switzerland).
- The sub-region R36 will have the capitals in Tyumen (Russia) and Kandahar (Afghanistan) - assistance from Nagoya (Japan).
- The sub-region R37 will have the capitals in Dushanbe (Tajikistan) and Labytnangi (Russia) - assistance from Limoges (France).
- The sub-region R38 will have the capitals in Astana (Kazakhstan) and Kabul (Afghanistan) - assistance from Rostock (Germany).
- The sub-region R39 will have the capitals in Islamabad (Pakistan) and Malé (Maldives) - assistance from La Rochelle (France).

Italy, Roma: Part of the Imperial Palaces (27 BC) on the Palatine Hill.

From Bishkek to Nagpur

SUN: Now region R4 is proud of its first 5 sub-regions.

EARTH: - The sub-region R40 will have the capitals in Bishkek (Kyrgyzstan) and Jaipur (India) - assistance from Osaka (Japan).
- The sub-region R41 will have the capitals in Akola (India) and Kashgar (China) - assistance from Genoa (Italy).
- The sub-region R42 will have the capitals in Almaty (Kazakhstan) and Coimbatore (India) - assistance from Perth (Australia).
- The sub-region R43 will have the capitals in Kuybyshev (Russia) and Agra (India) - assistance from Fukuoka (Japan).
- The sub-region R44 will have the capitals in Vertikos (Russia) and Nagpur (India) - assistance from Coral Bay (Australia).

France, Paris: Tour Eiffel (1889, 324 m, looking north-west): Tour Eiffel shadow (right), Pont d'Iéna over La Seine (center down), Jardin du Trocadéro (center), Chaillot Palace (middle), tall buildings in Courbevoie near La Seine (up center, 4.5 km away).

From Chennai to Tomsk

SUN: I am eager to see next 5 sub-regions, from the method.

EARTH: Here they are: - The sub-region R45 will have the capitals in Chennai (India) and Colombo (Sri Lanka) - assistance from Sapporo (Japan).
- The sub-region R46 will have the capitals in Lucknow (India) and Fedosikha (Russia) - assistance from Niigata (Japan).
- The sub-region R47 will have the capitals in Bilaspur (India) and Kolpashevo (Russia) - assistance from Albany (Australia).
- The sub-region R48 will have the capitals in Visakhapatnam (India) and Barnaul (Russia) - assistance from Hiroshima (Japan).
- The sub-region R49 will have the capitals in Brahmapur (India) and Tomsk (Russia) - assistance from Yokohama (Japan).

Italy, Roma: On Ponte Palatino (1891), the remaining arch of the Pons Aemilius (178 BC, Ponte Rotto, left), Pons Fabricius (62 BC, right).

From Kathmandu to Abakan

SUN: R4 is coming strong with its first 5 sub-regions.

EARTH: - The sub-region R50 will have the capitals in Kathmandu (Nepal) and Patna (India) - assistance from Kobe (Japan).
- The sub-region R51 will have the capitals in Bayingol (China) and Novokuznetsk (Russia) - assistance from Vichy (France).
- The sub-region R52 will have the capitals in Thimphu (Bhutan) and Dhaka (Bangladesh) - assistance from Jena (Germany).
- The sub-region R53 will have the capitals in Lhasa (China) and Achinsk (Russia) - assistance from Reims (France).
- The sub-region R54 will have the capitals in Abakan (Russia) and Kumul (China) - assistance from Fribourg (Switzerland).

Japan, Kyoto (678): the hall gate of the founder of the Shinshu Honbyo Temple (1321, until 1987 Higashi Hongan-Ji, total area 99,000 m^2, interior area 29,700 m^2), on the west side of Karasuma Dori, north of Shichijo Dori and south of Hanayacho Dori.

From Dibrugarh to Chiang Mai

SUN: The next 5 are so lovely, straight from the method.

EARTH: - The sub-region R55 will have the capitals in Kyzyl (Russia) and Dibrugarh (India) - assistance from Denmark (Australia).
- The sub-region R56 will have the capitals in Bassein (Myanmar) and Tinsukia (India) - assistance from Chiba (Japan).
- The sub-region R57 will have the capitals in Yushu City (China) and Tinskoy (Russia) - assistance from Klagenfurt (Austria).
- The sub-region R58 will have the capitals in Jiuquan (China) and Medan (Indonesia) - assistance from Lucerne (Switzerland).
- The sub-region R59 will have the capitals in Chiang Mai (Thailand) and Dehong (China) - assistance from Mulhouse (France).

Paris (250 BC), la Seine, the north-west end of l'Île de la Cité, Vedettes du Pont Neuf: the Parisis boat, the northern part of Pont Neuf (1578-1607, the oldest bridge in Paris).

From Bangkok to Ulan Bator

SUN: I am ready for the first 5 of R6.

EARTH: - The sub-region R60 will have the capitals in Bangkok (Thailand) and Kuala Lumpur (Malaysia) - assistance from Besançon (France).
- The sub-region R61 will have the capitals in Vientiane (Laos) and Singapore – assistance from Freiburg im Breisgau (Germany).
- The sub-region R62 will have the capitals in Phnom Penh (Cambodia) and Irkutsk (Russia) – assistance from Baden (Switzerland).
- The sub-region R63 will have the capitals in Palembang (Indonesia), Hanoi (Vietnam) – assistance from Thun (Switzerland).
- The sub-region R64 will have the capitals in Ulan Bator (Mongolia) and Ulan-Ude (Russia) – assistance from Chaumont (France).

USA: Chicago, 1837: from the Skydeck (floor 103, 412 m) of Willis Tower (1973, 108 floors, 527 m) a view of the south-east part of Chicago with Maurice Rothschild Bldg. (1928, 62 m, left), One Museum Park (2009, 221 m, center-right) and Lake Michigan.

From Cirebon to Hong Kong

SUN: The next 5 are irresistible.

EARTH: - The sub-region R65 will have the capitals in Cirebon (Indonesia) and Nanning (China) – assistance from Vaduz (Lichtenstein).
- The sub-region R66 will have the capitals in Pontianak (Indonesia) and Baotou (China) – assistance from Lugano (Switzerland).
- The sub-region R67 will have the capitals in Surakarta (Indonesia) and Yichang (China) – assistance from Thonon-les-Bain (France).
- The sub-region R68 will have the capitals in Surabaya (Indonesia) and Changsha (China) – assistance from Burgdorf (Switzerland).
- The sub-region R69 will have the capitals in Chita (Russia) and Hong Kong (China) – assistance from Colmar (France).

Italy, Roma: The south side of the Arch (315) of Constantine (272 – 337, Roman Emperor 306 - 337), from Via di San Gregorio.

From Nanchang to Kupang

SUN: Let's see now the marvelous first 5 of R7, from the great Method.

EARTH: - The sub-region R70 will have the capitals in Bandar Seri Begawan (Brunei Darussalam) and Nanchang (China) – assistance from Turku (Finland).
- The sub-region R71 will have the capitals in Krasnokamensk (Russia) and Jinan (China) – assistance from St. Gallen (Switzerland).
- The sub-region R72 will have the capitals in Baguio City (Philippines) and Hangzhou (China) – assistance from Dole (France).
- The sub-region R73 will have the capitals in Manila (Philippines) and Taipei (Taiwan, China) – assistance from Metz (France).
- The sub-region R74 will have the capitals in Kupang (Indonesia) and Shanghai (China) – assistance from Davos (Switzerland).

Paris (250 BC), on Quai de l'Horloge: Pont au Change (1860, Napoleon III), Théâtre de la Ville (1862, by Baron Haussmann at Place du Châtelet), la Tour Saint-Jacques (1508, on Rue de Rivoli).

From Pyongyang to Melbourne

SUN: Naturally, the next 5 sub-regions are full of splendor, like the method itself.

EARTH: - The sub-region R75 will have the capitals in Pyongyang (North Korea) and Seoul (South Korea) – assistance from Versailles (France).
- The sub-region R76 will have the capitals in Vladivostok (Russia) and Busan (South Korea) – assistance from Innsbruck (Austria).
- The sub-region R77 will have the capitals in Kyoto (Japan) and Khabarovsk (Russia) – assistance from Germering (Germany).
- The sub-region R78 will have the capitals in Nagoya (Japan) and Komsomolsk-on-Amur (Russia) – assistance from Venice (Italy).
- The sub-region R79 will have the capitals in Sendai (Japan) and Melbourne (Australia) – assistance from St. Moritz (Switzerland).

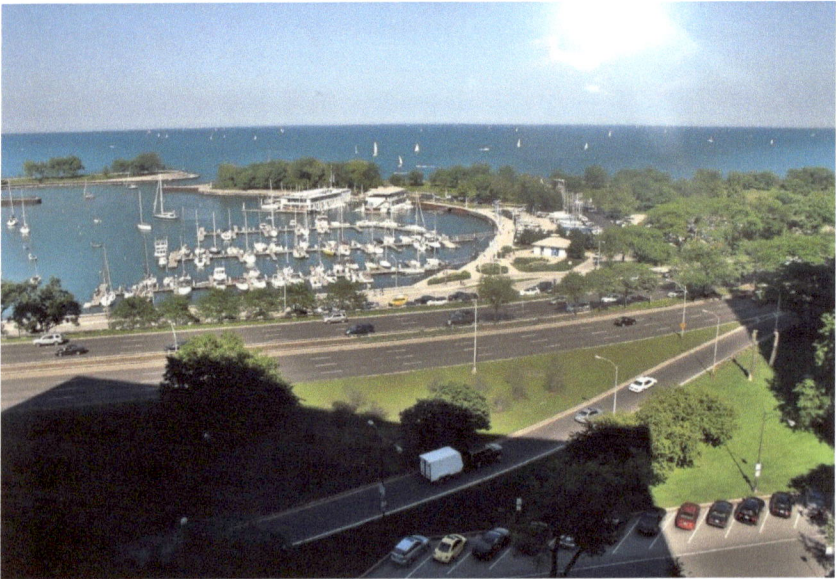

USA: Chicago, 1837: from an apartment at the 6th floor in 3180 North Lake Shore Drive residential Building (1952, 23 floors, 72 m), near West Belmont Avenue, a view of the south marina from the Belmont Harbor on Lake Michigan.

From Anchorage to Hermosillo

SUN: It's time to cross the Pacific – the first 5 sub-regions of R8.

EARTH: The sub-region R80 will have the capitals in Uelen (Russia) and Anchorage (Alaska, USA), – assistance from Zug (Switzerland).
- The sub-region R81 will have the capitals in Vancouver (Canada) and San Jose (CA, USA) – assistance from Odense (Denmark).
- The sub-region R82 will have the capitals in Vernon (Canada) and Los Angeles (CA, USA) – assistance from Amstetten (Austria).
- The sub-region R83 will have the capitals in Calgary (Canada) and Tijuana (Mexico) – assistance from Chur (Switzerland).
- The sub-region R84 will have the capitals in Hermosillo (Mexico) and Tucson (AR, USA) – assistance from Bergen (Norway).

The south-west side of the Amphitheatrum Flavium (80 AD, Colosseum, right), built by Vespasian Flavius and his son Titus.

From Regina to Lima

SUN: The next 5 sub-regions will bring us to the Atlantic.

EARTH: The sub-region R85 will have the capitals in Chihuahua (Mexico) and Regina (Canada) – assistance from Gothenburg (Sweden).
- The sub-region R86 will have the capitals in San Luis Potosi City (Mexico) and Winnipeg (Canada) – assistance from Yverdon-les-Bains (Switzerland).
- The sub-region R87 will have the capitals in Tulsa (OK, USA) and Veracruz (Mexico) – assistance from Bregenz (Austria).
- The sub-region R88 will have the capitals in Memphis (TN, USA) and San José (Costa Rica) – assistance from Uppsala (Sweden).
- The sub-region R89 will have the capitals in Lima (Peru) and Boston (MA, USA) – assistance from Tampere (Finland).

France, Paris: La Seine, on Parisis boat: the northern part of Pont (or Passerelle) des Arts (1802-1804, Napoleon, 1981-1984, 155 m by 11m, left), the south-east side of Musée du Louvre (1793).

From Bangor to Cayenne

SUN: Let's see the very interesting first 5 sub-regions of R9.

EARTH: - The sub-region R90 will have the capitals in La Paz (Bolivia) and Bangor (Maine, USA) – assistance from Aosta (Italy).
- The sub-region R91 will have the capitals in Caracas (Venezuela) and Road Town (British Virgin Islands) – assistance from Obergoms (Switzerland).
- The sub-region R92 will have the capitals in Buenos Aires (Argentina) and Fort-de-France (Martinique) – assistance from Freudenstadt (Germany).
- The sub-region R93 will have the capitals in Asuncion (Paraguay) and Montevideo (Uruguay) – assistance from Winterthur (Switzerland).
- The sub-region R94 will have the capitals in Cayenne (French Guiana), St. John's (Canada) – assistance from Novara (Italy).

Japan, Kyoto (678): detail of the hall gate of the founder of the Shinshu Honbyo Temple (1321, until 1987 Higashi Hongan-Ji, total area 99,000 m^2, interior area 29,700 m^2), on Karasuma Dori, north of Shichijo Dori and south of Hanayacho Dori.

From Rio de Janeiro to London

SUN: Finally, pour la bonne bouche, how the method says, the inviting last 5 sub-regions.

EARTH: - The sub-region R95 will have the capitals in Rio de Janeiro (Brazil) and Dakar (Senegal) – assistance from Toyama (Japan).
- The sub-region R96 will have the capitals in Freetown (Sierra Leone) and Lisbon (Portugal) – assistance from Kawasaki (Japan).
- The sub-region R97 will have the capitals in Bamako (Mali) and Athlone (Ireland) – assistance from Ulm (Germany).
- The sub-region R98 will have the capitals in Yamoussoukro (Cote d'Ivoire) and Madrid (Spain) – assistance from Okayama (Japan).
- The sub-region R99 will have the capitals in Ouagadougou (Burkina Faso) and London (United Kingdom) - assistance from Vaasa (Finland).

Temple of Saturn (42 BC, center-left up), Curia (283, center up), Nerva's Forum (97, down), Forum Caesaris (46 BC, center-right).

61

DM25.3. Level 3 Management

SUN: What the method says about the management of the ten regions?

EARTH: Ten L3 friendly managers for the 10 regions will supervise and assist the 10 L2 managers of the 10 sub-regions of each region, for a total of about 770,000,000 people for each region.

Paris, Île de la Cité: the oldest public clock in France (left, built in 1370 with a mechanism from 1334), at the north-est corner of La Conciergerie, the Palace of French Kings from 950 until 1358.

DM25.4. Level 4 Management

SUN: Now let's see what Dediu Method recommends for the top management of the world.

EARTH: Yes, the method clearly states that the L4 level very friendly 10 Advisers of the world will supervise and assist the 10 L3 managers of the 10 regions of the Earth, for a total of over 7,700,000,000 people – all the people on Earth, citizens of Peaceful Terra.

Japan, Kyoto (678): the hall gate (right) of the founder of the Shinshu Honbyo Temple (1321), on Karasuma Dori, looking south, with Kyoto Tower (1964, 131 m, observation deck 100 m).

Locations

SUN: And what the method mentions about where will they be located?

EARTH: The method insists that the L4 very friendly 10 Advisers of the world will be located each in one the ten Regions R0, R1,…, R9. For example, in the beginning, for the first month (then changing every month), the ten Advisers of the world will be located:

- in R0: Barcelona (Spain)
- in R1: Benghazi (Libya)
- in R2: Addis Ababa (Ethiopia)
- in R3: Hyderabad (Pakistan)
- in R4: Bhopal (India)
- in R5: Mandalay (Myanmar)
- in R6: Nanchong (China)
- in R7: Khabarovsk (Russia)
- in R8: Houston (USA)
- in R9: Recife (Brazil)

Paris, Île de la Cité: the oldest public clock in France, built in 1370 with a mechanism from 1334, adorned with the statues of Piety (left) and Justice (right), on the front of the Tour de l'Horloge (1350 – 1353, 47 m high, at the north-east corner of La Conciergerie, the Palace of French Kings from 950 until 1358 when they moved to Louvre), at the corner of the Palais de Justice, on Boulevard du Palais at the junction with Quai de l'Horloge, in the 1er Arrondissement, 350 m north-west of Notre Dame (1345).

The best management of the world

SUN: And how will they work for the benefit of all people, according to the method?

EARTH: Very important indeed: these ten L4 Advisers will be in permanent contact with each other, and with the L3 Advisers, for the best management of the world.

The ten L4 Advisers will work by consensus only.

The ten L4 Advisers will be elected from the 10 regions, and each of them will be the First Adviser (***First among equals*** – from Latin: Primus inter pares) for one month, by rotation.

The First Adviser only coordinates the work of the other 9 Advisors for one month.

Canada, Niagara Falls: the American Falls (21-30 m drop, 290 m wide), the Bridal Veil Falls (right, 21m), after Luna Island.

Mobility

SUN: Are these 10 Advisers fixed in some places?

EARTH: No, the method mentions that the ten L4 Advisers will move each month from a first capital of a region to the second capital of another region, at random (or based on urgency, if an emergency occurred). This mobility is essential for having a long period of tranquility and harmony.

For example, in this COVID-19 case, they all would have focused on the initial cases, help the local management to isolate the people affected, give them proper medical assistance, and stop the local travel. All the medical institutions in the world would work together to find a quick solution to this new medical problem, and, obviously, all the people would get the best protection and assistance.

Italy, Roma: Curia (283, left up), Forum Nervae (97, down), Forum Caesaris (46 BC, center, Julius Caesar 100 BC – 44 BC), Altare della Patria.

DM26. Monthly World Report

SUN: Will these Advisors present regular short reports to the people, according to the method?

EARTH: Yes, the First Adviser, on the last day of each month, will present in writing for the world (no more than 5 standard pages) a clear and precise Monthly World Report, with a list of finished and unfinished tasks. The other 9 Advisers will add their comments to the Monthly World Report (no more than half a page each - total report less than 9.5 pages).

France, Paris: La Seine, on Parisis boat: the east side of the Galeries des Antiques (south building) of Musée du Louvre (1793).

DM26.1. Replacements

SUN: What the method suggests about management and replacements?

EARTH: The top 10 Advisers will manage Police and all other Departments. For obvious uncooperative or improper attitude of one top Advisor X, the other 9 can replace X with X's number 2, and X will receive appropriate medical treatment. When vacancies happen for Advisors, the number 2 for those Advisors will fill the vacancies. All the activities of all Advisors will be recorded in computers and videos, and on paper, for people to be able to see what they are doing. Advisors at all levels should work 40 hours/week, with 4 weeks vacation, but many services (medical, police (firemen should be part of the police), emergency, volunteers) should be non-stop.

Chicago, 1837: from an apartment in 3180 North Lake Shore Drive Bldg. (1952, 23 fl, 72 m), near W Belmont Ave, a view of the south part of Belmont Harbor (left) on Lake Michigan, and of 3150 North Lake Shore Drive Bldg. (1963, 38 fl, 103 m, right).

DM26.2. Spending proposals

SUN: Based on the method, compensation of the world government employees is relevant.

EARTH: Yes, the world government employees will have a compensation close to the average compensation of the people in the area where they are located, but the top management will a compensation close to the world average. All Advisors are free to speak about their administrative work, but only with modesty – people will evaluate their work. All spending proposals from Advisers must be approved by their 5 assistants (doctors, mathematicians, CEOs, engineers and teachers), and must have an already existing funding in the budget.

Italy, Roma: Templum Saturni (42 BC, right up), the Column of Phocas (608, center-right), Basilica Aemilia (Marcus Aemilius, 179 BC, down).

DM27. No war

SUN: Dediu Method is very insistent on this - who can declare war?

EARTH: Nobody! Advisors (and all the others) cannot declare war, reprisals or capture land or water. Advisors (and all the others) cannot raise and support armies, navy, or any military forces.

SUN: Seneca (circa 1,960 years ago) surprises us with his aphorism: "Man is something sacred for man".

EARTH: Yes, we must retain this excellent aphorism, and apply it every day – the results will be phenomenal! There are people who were born with birth defects – with careful medical treatment they can be transformed in healthy people.

SUN: Rousseau (over 250 years ago) is brilliant…..

EARTH: Yes, "Force does not constitute right... obedience is due only to legitimate powers". For thousands of years many tried to impose obedience by force, but always failed. Now people want to get rid of this bad habit. Also, Rousseau: "Insults are the arguments employed by those who are in the wrong." We still see this daily, but the people will change this soon.

SUN: The very impressive Plato (over 2,370 years ago)…..

EARTH: Yes, "When the tyrant has disposed of foreign enemies by conquest or treaty, and there is nothing more to fear from them, then he is always stirring up some war or other, in order that the people may require a leader." It is so right all the time.

France, Paris: The sculpture "Lyric Drama" (1868 – 1869, 4 m by 2.3 m, by Jean-Joseph Perraud (1819 – 1876, he enjoyed a great reputation during the Second Empire – Napoleon III, 1852 - 1870), on the right side of the right outer bay on the façade of l'Opéra de Paris (1875), which is the most famous opera house in the world, and a prestigious symbol of Paris.

DM28. Public opinion survey

SUN: Will the people be involved in the world government?

EARTH: Certainly - in order to better know the world government, to help it, and, especially, to improve it, all able people of the world will work as volunteers at least one day per year in each of the seven departments.

Also, after each Monthly World Report, a public opinion survey about the report should be taken, and presented to all Advisors. All activities of the Advisors, and others from the small World Government, will be available to the people on a website.

The top 10 Advisers (and all the others) will collaborate via e-mail, telephone, videoconferences, mail, or face to face, when needed, to produce practical results for all people, very fast.

Japan, Kyoto (678): the hall gate of the founder of the Shinshu Honbyo Temple (1321, until 1987 Higashi Hongan-Ji, total area 99,000 m^2), viewed from a round water garden in the middle of Karasuma Dori, north of Shichijo Dori, south of Hanayacho Dori.

DM29. Five assistants

SUN: Now, another major idea from Dediu Method: who will help the Advisors to manage the world?

EARTH: Very important indeed - each Advisor, and each manager at all levels, will have 5 immediate assistants:
1) a mathematician for finance and all other calculations,
2) a medical doctor for keeping everybody healthy, calm, polite, friendly and optimist,
3) a CEO for good management,
4) an engineer for all practical projects, and
5) a teacher for education, training and related areas.

The five assistants play a key role, because they are highly qualified professionals, who actually will carry on the practical management of the world. Their integrity, professionalism and friendliness will significantly improve the quality of the world and local governments.

The five assistants are really the experts. They will assist the Advisors and all levels of management, in order to have an efficient, correct and professional working of the world government at all levels.

Japan, Tokyo: Shinjuku, one of the 23 special wards of Tokyo, with Shinjuku Mitsui Building (224 m, 55 floors, 1974, left), Shinjuku Center Building (223 m, 54 floors, 1979, center), Mode Gakuen Cocoon Tower (204 m, 50 floors, 2008, center-right).

Tokyo started around 1150 as a small fishing village named Edo (which means estuary). Edo was first fortified by the Edo clan, around 1180. In 1457 Edo Castle was built. In 1590 Tokugawa Ieyasu transformed Edo into his base and later, in 1603, the town became the center of his nationwide military government. Between 1603 and 1868 (Edo period), the city Edo developed into one of the biggest cities in the world, with a population of over one million by 1700. Its name was changed to Tokyo (east capital) when it became the imperial capital in 1868.

The population of the main city is over 9 million people; with the closest suburbs the total population exceeds 13 millions. The world's most populous metropolitan area is Tokyo, with circa 35 million people, and it also is the world's largest urban agglomeration economy, with a GDP of $1.479 trillion at purchasing power parity. The city is home for 51 of the Fortune Global 500 companies, the highest number for any city. The tallest structure in Tokyo is Tokyo Skytree (a lattice tower, 634 m, 2012).

DM30. Honorific World Observer

SUN: Aesop, over 2,590 years ago, said it right: "In union there is strength."

EARTH: Yes, for this we need to unite all 7.7 billions of people in a harmonious country Peaceful Terra, all focusing on peace, freedom, good health, good education, and prosperity for everybody.

SUN: Another structural idea from Dediu Method: who oversees the Advisers?

EARTH: An Honorific World Observer will be quietly elected by direct vote – starting, for example, 1st September 2022 - for only one 3 years term, with the main duty to observe that the top 10 Advisers efficiently perform their duties, and keep their words – if they don't, they will be changed.

For managers and for everybody else, keeping their word is a serious and strict requirement.

The Honorific World Observer has this responsibility for the top 10 Advisors, but all people will pay attention to this. Words must become again important and respected.

Canada, Niagara Falls: Niagara SkyWheel in Dinosaur Park and Miniature Golf, near Clifton Hill and Oneida Lane, 1.5 km north of the Horseshoe Falls.

DM31. World Government

SUN: Jefferson, over 200 years ago, was right….

EARTH: "Whenever you do a thing, act as if the entire world were watching" – this is exactly what every government employee should have in mind.

SUN: New ideas from Dediu Method about the World Government.

EARTH: - Yes - all the employees of the World Government are temporary, and must reapply for their positions every year. There is no need for unions. If the world government have complaints, they will discuss them with any of the advisors, or specialists from the People Assistance Department – if there are management abuses or errors, they will promptly be corrected, and the work will continue for people's benefit.

The World Government will be limited to:
1) the Office of the Honorific Observer (less than 10 employees),
2) the Office of the top ten Advisors (less than 100 employees), and
3) 7 small departments, with less than 3,000,000 employees.

The number of all government employees, at all levels, will be less than 350,000,000, and at the top level less than 3,000,000.

SUN: Dediu Method precisely defines just 7 departments.

EARTH: Yes, the World Government will have these 7 small departments:

DM 31.1. Tax Department – 15% tax

- Collects taxes of 15% of the income of people and revenue of companies.

- The Manager of the Tax Department is appointed for a three-year term by the World 10 Advisers.

- The number of employees must be under 50,000, with excellent computers, and advanced software.

France, Paris: La Seine, on Parisis boat, looking downriver: Pont du Carrousel, 1831-1834, between the Place du Carrousel (part of Musée du Louvre (1793), right) and the Quai Voltaire (left).

SUN: Yes, 15% tax is a clear idea, let's see the next.

EARTH: The next is

DM 31.2. Treasury – with many new tasks

Treasury will control all the financial issues, including:
- antitrust
- fiscal service
- financial cooperation
- financing bank
- world reserve system
- world budget using only revenue, no borrowing, and spending only on strict necessary needs
– all the budgets, at all levels, will have a 2% surplus, which will be returned to the taxpayers
- register of all government papers and activities
- archives and records
- assist all people to have savings accounts for old age (the old age will be starting around 70), and 10% of their income should automatically go to their savings accounts. For those unable to work, their doctors and mathematicians will decide case by case.
- bankruptcies, in general, will be discouraged, and when strict necessary, will be analyzed and solved, case by case, by the doctors, mathematicians and CEOs who worked with the people who asked the bankruptcy.
- encourage all families to assist their parents, grandparents, and great-grandparents.
- housing finance
- housing for all people
- no homelessness
- consumer financial protection
- pensions
- privacy
- current social security until replaced by personal savings
- personnel management
- general services for the world government

- each the 10 regions will receive 2.5% of the world taxes - at least 30% of the money will be sent to villages and cities.

- each of the 100 sub-regions will receive 0.25% of the world taxes. At least 40% of the money will be sent to villages and cities.

- The World Central Bank will include all current central banks – starting, for example, on May 1st, 2023.

- The Special Credit Card (SCC) will be issued by the World Central Bank.

- Advisors will create a new world currency, named, for example, "coin", and all the other currencies will be exchanged for coins. The World Central Bank will implement the details.

- The counterfeiting and all other bad things, which some sick people do, will be medically treated (in specialized medical institutions when necessary), and those who did bad things will pay all the expenses, and will reimburse the victims. Victims will always be very protected, and helped to recover the losses from the attackers.

Japan: A building with a modern amphitheater at Tokyo Denki University (TDU, founded in 1907) in the north-east of the Inzai (Chiba) campus, in Muzai-Gakuendai, 34 km north-east of Tokyo.

SUN: Treasury has plenty of important tasks – let's see the next.

EARTH: Yes, the next Department is

DM31.3. People Assistance Department - new

It will assist people in general, including:
- parent assistance
- dispute resolution
- in very simple disputes or culpa levis (ordinary negligence, like late payments, etc.), one single assistant will decide within minutes, and all people will go back to work
- census very 5 years
- election assistance every 20 months
 - special credit cards
- people protection against abuses from anybody
- completely eliminate corruption, organized crime and drug trafficking
- all people in the world will remain in their places, and the improvements will come to them. Those who want to move to other places, will need first a special invitation from at least 10 people (not family related) where they want to move.
- all the Tribunals and related areas will be transformed in people assistance services, based on friendliness, collaboration and goodwill.
- It is well understood that no excessive bail will be required, no excessive fines imposed, no cruel and unusual punishments applied, but, at the same time, it is well understood that a person who did a bad thing will receive the necessary corrective medical treatment, and will reimburse all people who suffered damages, and the medical treatment. The victims will always receive special attention.
- Nobility (King, Prince, etc.) could continue to exist in some places, but they should not interfere with activities of the Advisors, and actually should help them.
- food safety
- trash & recycling
- free commerce
- jobs assistance

- postal service
- labor safety and harmonious relations
- land, water
- volunteers
- fitness, sport, tourism
- 10 world holidays: the normal 4 Earth events (2 solstices (around 21 June, around 21 December), and 2 equinoxes (around 21 March, around 21 September), Mother's Day on 1st May, Father's Day on 6 August, Children's Day on 6 November, Grandparents' Day on 6 February, and 2 optional days (like Thanksgiving or a Religious Day (Christmas), and New Year).

Canada, Niagara Falls: Niagara River after the Horseshoe Falls (in Canada, 53 m drop, 790 m wide).

SUN: Very good people assistance – let's see the next.

EARTH: Yes – the next Department is

DM31.4. Medical Department – many new tasks

It will manage all medical and healthcare related areas, including:
- human services
- conflict resolution
- families, children, elderly
- medicine approval
- disease control and prevention
- medical doctors and assistants will make regular home visits, at least once a year, to all people, to keep them healthy, and to prevent illnesses.
- medical research: cancer, heart, lung, blood, arthritis, surgical robotics, connected computers for healthcare, etc.
- healthy homes, streets, stores, working places, etc.
- healthy aging
- all misunderstandings, disagreements or conflicts of any nature will be treated by medical personnel (with police help when strict necessary), until all is back to normal.
- no prisons are necessary, only specialized medical institutions (in simple cases, the places where the treated people live can be used, with the necessary limitations and surveillance)
- If a person X is considered that did a bad thing, X will have, within 3 days, a discussion with one or more doctors and other assistants, and will be informed of the nature and cause of the bad thing; including witnesses against and for him. Then a decision will be taken within other 3 days, by a group of doctors and other assistants. Victims of bad people will always have priority to discuss their problems with one or more doctors and other assistants, and quick decisions will be taken within 3 days, by a group of doctors and other assistants. Protection of victims has always priority.
- in order to better know the world government, to help it, and, especially, to improve it, all able people of the world will work as

volunteers at least one day per year in the local facility of this department, which will have a special office for managing this volunteer work.

– all people will have government medical insurance, and they can also have private medical insurance

– there will be doctors working for the government 100%, or only part-time, or having only private practice, all with reasonable salaries and fees.

– there will be government pharmaceutical institutions and private pharmaceutical companies, offering reasonable priced medicines, without advertising to the general public.

France, Paris: La Seine, on Parisis boat, looking to the left bank: Musée d'Orsay (1986, former Gare d'Orsay (1898-1900)), on Rue de la Légion d'Honneur, Quai Anatole France, near Port de Solférino.

SUN: As we can see from the COVID-19 pandemic, this World Medical Department is a high priority – the sooner you have it, the better.

EARTH: Indeed, we need to work very hard for this. The next Department is

DM31.5. Police – with many new tasks

Police will provide assistance for:
- accidents
- disasters
- complete elimination of nuclear, chemical and biological arms, firearms and explosives
- world complete security
- world cooperation
- conflict reduction and resolution
- investigations
- emergency assistance
- training
- delinquency prevention in general, and especially juvenile
- protection of Advisors, important government buildings, etc.
- extended surveillance and reconnaissance to prevent bad events
- fire protection
- volunteers to help police
- police will be present at public meetings, services, shows, etc., in order to protect the public
- public order
- ensuring traffic safety
- completely eliminate corruption, organized crime and drug trafficking
- movement of people based on civilized rules
- assist and protect those who have encountered violence
- World Police and specialists from the former United Nations and Interpol will be ready and very mobile for urgent and special operations, when they are needed.

- Police will be the only department which will have some small arms, in order to stop some very bad people (who are very sick).
- a small manufacturing and maintenance of arms unit will be part of the Police Department, under strict control.
- Police will work with medical personnel, mathematicians, CEOs, engineers, teachers and others, to make sure that all the people on the Planet are in good mental health, in order to prevent bad situations. This is also a major responsibility of all Advisors.
- prevention of bad events
- The Advisors will allocate the necessary budget for Police, and Police will assist people in need.

Japan: Tsutaya store in front of the Inzai Post Office, 300 m north-est from the entrance to the Inzai (Chiba) campus of Tokyo Denki University (TDU, founded in 1907) in Muzai-Gakuendai, 34 km north-east of Tokyo.

SUN: it is well-known that always there is need for Police, because of accidents, etc. And the 6th Department?

EARTH: Yes, we have the

DM31.6 Education Department – with vital changes

- Over 2 billions of children in the world will get a solid peace-oriented education, to give a solid peace-oriented foundation for a good, free, peaceful and prosperous life.
- Education is very important – teachers will work with parents and grandparents, to educate the children to leave healthy in a sustainable peace, liberty and prosperity.
- Discipline must be strict, and those who do not behave properly, will get medical assistance.
- The world will have 4 school levels (SLs) of education:
SL1 – Kindergarten – 2 years: age 5 and 6
SL2 – Primary School – 4 years: age 7, 8, 9 and 10
SL3 – Secondary School – 3 years: age 11, 12 and 13
SL4 – High School or Vocational School – 4 years: age 14, 15, 16 and 17
- A World Library will include the Library of Congress and all the other great libraries – they will remain where they are now, but will be digitally interconnected, and accessible from any place in the world.
- adult education: technical, career
- training for employment
- management training
- post high school education
- peace education
- world constitution education

SUN: Do you remember Benjamin Franklin (over 240 years ago)?

EARTH: Certainly, "An investment in knowledge pays the best interest." Therefore, good education at all levels and at all ages, pays the best interest for everybody.

SUN: Pliny the Elder (circa 1,950 years ago) said in Latin: *Nemo mortalium omnibus horis sapit.*

EARTH: "No mortal is wise at all times." For this we need to frequently change the management, bring better people with better ideas and with more energy to work hard. When mistakes are done, recognize them, apologize, and immediately correct them. And Beethoven, about 200 years ago, said it right: "Nothing is more intolerable than to have to admit to yourself your own errors."

SUN: Hoover (circa 60 years ago) is astonishingly right…

EARTH: Yes, "Peace is not made at the council table or by treaties, but in the hearts of men". Exactly this is the purpose of all the education, news, media, shows, movies, meetings, etc.

SUN: The good Arthur Schopenhauer (over 170 years ago) is waiting…..

EARTH: Yes, "Without books the development of civilization would have been impossible. They are the engines of change, windows on the world, "Lighthouses" as the poet said "erected in the sea of time." They are companions, teachers, magicians, bankers of the treasures of the mind. Books are humanity in print." We do need plenty of good books about peace, freedom and harmony. Schopenhauer also said: "Talent hits a target no one else can hit; Genius hits a target no one else can see."

Paris (250 BC), the north-west part of l'Île de la Cité, on Quai de l'Horloge: Cour de Cassation (1791) is in the Palais de Justice. A Roman fort was in this part in 361, when Julian the Apostate (330-363) was proclaimed Roman Emperor. Philippe Auguste (1165-1223) made it his residence and invited Richard I (the Lionheart) (1157-1199) here. His grandson, Louis IX (1214-1270), built the Sainte Chapelle nearby, from 1242 to 1248.

SUN: No need to repeat how important the education of children is for the future of the world. And the 7th Department?

EARTH: Yes, this is relatively new:

31.7. Science & Technology Department.

It will help in the areas of:
- mathematics
- statistics
- science
- technology
- Algorithmic Governance will be an essential tool for a better and impartial governing of the world, used by the Advisers elected by people. Mathematicians from all countries will work to improve the Algorithmic Governance, to better serve the people.
- cyberspace complete security will be achieved and strictly maintained
- information systems
- computer services
- Internet
- scientific cooperation
- economic development at the world level
- infrastructure improvement and maintenance at the world level
- innovation and improvements in all areas, at the world level
- transportation at the world level
- safety
- security
- aviation
- highway
- cars
- railroads without noise
- maritime administration
- logistics
- strategic planning at the world level
- public works
- fleet maintenance

- standards: weights, measures, etc.
- research at the world level
- risk analysis
- laboratories
- engineering
- communications at the world level
- telecommunications
- networks
- peaceful nuclear energy use at the world level
- safety
- waste
- electrical power
- oceanic analysis at the world level
- atmospheric analysis at the global level
- meteorological service and prognosis at the global level
- world resources analysis
- sustainable use of world resources
- geographical and geological activity
- product safety at the global level
- hazardous material and chemical safety
- government broadcasting (radio, tv, Internet, newspaper, etc.) including news, scientific and technical information
- private broadcasting will continue, but the world government must be able to directly inform the people, without intermediaries
- space exploration and expansion at the world level – very important for the future
- patent and trademark
- intellectual rights
- all government work, which can be done by private companies, will be contracted with the best and reasonably priced private companies. At the same time, the government should always have competitive services for people – from plumbing and electrical help, to mortgage and buying or selling a house.

SUN: Louis Pasteur, over 130 years ago, had a clear idea of one country on Earth, with peace, freedom, good health, and strong science.

EARTH: Yes, "Science knows no country, because knowledge belongs to humanity, and is the torch which illuminates the world". We continue his ideas, and we will implement these good ideas, for the benefit of humanity.

Wind turbine working on the north-west part of the Inzai (Chiba) campus of Tokyo Denki University, 34 km north-east of Tokyo.

DM32. Elections – very different

SUN: Well, this World Science & Technology Department is a sine qua non requirement for a modern Earth. Now some more information on elections. You remember Plato (over 2,370 years ago), don't you?

EARTH: Sure: "Access to power must be confined to those who are not in love with it." The Advisers should be elected every 20 months for one term only. If an Adviser X was elected for a term T1, then the next term T2 will have another Advisor Y. For the next term T3, X can be elected again, but the next term T4 will have a new Adviser, and so on. All levels of Advisers (minimum age 25 years) can be elected, not consecutively, at most 4 times (maximum 80 months = 6 years and 8 months).

SUN: Will the Government employees follow some well-established advice?

EARTH: Certainly - all the employees in Government will respect Seneca's (circa 1,960 years ago) aphorism "To govern is to serve, not to rule", and Hippocrates' (over 2,400 years ago) aphorisms "Make a habit of two things: to help; or at least to do no harm" and "Everything in excess is opposed to nature."

SUN: Will the elections be similar to what they are now?

EARTH: Not at all - Advisers should have exceptional results obtained from their work, and based on these results, plus modesty, moderation, good character, friendliness, sharp mind, wisdom, good morals, and intense desire to help people, they will be elected, without any campaigning, publicity, fundraising, donations, debates, propaganda, political parties, advertising, or similar activities.

SUN: And it is good to have in mind Thucydides, over 2,430 years ago…

EARTH: "Ignorance is bold and knowledge reserved."

SUN: Now Plato (over 2,370 years ago)….

EARTH: Yes, "Any man may easily do harm, but not every man can do good to another." Exactly this is the major issue which must be solved – everybody must understand not to do harm, and then to try to do good to others. When we achieve this objective, the long-term harmony is with us. Also:
"Excess generally causes reaction, and produces a change in the opposite direction, whether it be in the seasons, or in individuals, or in governments." This happened numerous times, but some still cannot understand.

Japan Kawaguchi city, near Kawaguchiko (Lake Kawaguchi, 6 km², 830 m elevation, left), 100 km south-west of Tokyo.

DM33. Digital technology

SUN: Other details, for a smooth transition?

EARTH: Yes - there will be use of advanced digital technology, which opens up entirely new opportunities for developing direct elections, and public control of the institutions, improving the transparency of the election procedure, and taking into account the interests and opinions of each voter (over the age of 21, who are not in a special medical institution for bad behavior or for mental health).

An Election Commission of 110 representatives from the 10 regions and from the 100 sub-regions, elected separately for 5 years, will have to examine the qualifications of all the candidates for Advisers, and for other senior management positions. Unqualified candidates will be asked to improve their qualifications, and then to try again later.

It is important to refresh the management, and to bring new people to help the big family of 7.7 B people. The older generations, who performed well, will be retained in important roles, because experience and maturity count very much. At least two months before the retirement, they will kindly be asked to transfer their expertise to the younger generation. Even after retirement, they will occasionally be invited to share their expertise.

In every election, with every winner, will be other two for number 2 and number 3. The number 2 and number 3 for each management position will be used when number 1 is not available (vacation, sick, etc.). They will constantly work for number 1, helping to solve urgent problems for the people.

SUN: Plato (over 2,370 years ago) again reminds us the truth....

EARTH: "He who is not a good servant, will not be a good master." The Election Commission will have to carefully examine this detail for all the candidates.

France: On the façade of l'Opéra de Paris (1875): a statue and the bust of Domenico Cimarosa (1749 – 1801), Italian opera composer, who wrote more than 80 operas, including Il matrimonio segreto (1792, written in Vienna, where he was invited by Emperor Leopold II (1747 – 1792); Giuseppe Verdi (1813 – 1901) considered it the model opera buffa), Il maestro di capella (1793), Semiramide (1799), Le astuzie femminili (1794), Le nozze di Lauretta (1797).

DM34. Useful new method

SUN: Good elections are essential for the future, and Dediu Method (as explained in this book and the previous books) is really useful.

EARTH: Indeed - there has been a tendency to make elections conflict generating events, with lots of propaganda, false information, heavy donations, unpolite confrontations, bully fundraising, hostile political parties and organizations, unlimited power ambitions, etc.

Using Dediu Method this will be completely changed into clean, friendly elections, in which people choose between leaders with outstanding results, plus talent to lead people to peace and freedom, modesty, moderation, good character, friendliness, sharp mind, wisdom, good morals, and intense desire to help people – no campaigning, no publicity, no fundraising, no donations, no debates, no propaganda, no political parties, no advertising, or similar activities.   All Advisors should also be local Administrators – they must show that they are good managers, and produce practical results for all people.

USA: Chicago, 1837: from the Skydeck (floor 103, 412 m) of Willis Tower (1973, 108 floors, 527 m) a view of the south-east part of Chicago, with One Financial Place Bldg. (1985, 39 fl, 157 m, down left) and Lake Michigan (left up).

DM35. World referendum

SUN: Electronic world referendum is another essential element of Dediu Method.

EARTH: Yes, an electronic world referendum will be organized every three months. The main questions will be:

1. Are you satisfied with the Government?
2. What Government work is good?
3. What Government work is not good?
4: Suggestions for improvement:

Within two months after each referendum, the Government will respond to the people. Based on the suggestions received, new pro-people rules will be replacing some old rules.

SUN: Confucius (circa 2,500 years ago) is always with us…..

EARTH: "Do not impose on others, what you yourself do not desire." Very important for all people in management. Also, this Confucius' aphorism: "He acts before he speaks, and afterwards speaks according to his actions."

DM36. Complete disarmament

SUN: Total and complete disarmament is a fundamental element of Dediu Method.

EARTH: Yes, arms will not exist anymore, and only police will have some small arms. Those who want arms for hunting or sport, will borrow them from police stations, with proper documents, rules and payments.

All military units will become strong civilian organizations, working to improve the quality of life for everybody.

For practical reasons, the transition from the current imperfect situation to the much better Sustainable Peace and Prosperity Structure (SPPS) will be very smooth: first - all the countries remain as they are, and they will begin – for example on January 1st, 2021 - to negotiate total and complete disarmament, with the help of the United Nations, for 3 months. Then for 5 months will intensely work to eliminate all the arms – either transform them in peaceful tools, or destroy them. Then a continuous verification and monitoring will be implemented, to make sure that the world finally achieved complete disarmament forever!

SUN: Churchill, over 60 years ago, said astoundingly correct things…

EARTH: Yes, "If the human race wishes to have a prolonged and indefinite period of material prosperity, they have only got to behave in a peaceful and helpful way toward one another". You see, this is what we are doing now! Churchill also helps us with this:
"If we open a quarrel between past and present, we shall find that we have lost the future". And with these:
"If you go on with this nuclear arms race, all you are going to do is make the rubble bounce".
"If you have ten thousand regulations, you destroy all respect for the law".

DM37. Census

SUN: What about census?

EARTH: A census will take place every 5 years – starting, for example, on October 1st, 2023 - and now we apply Dediu Method: all people will receive a special credit card (SCC), with their photo and other personal data. The delimitations between regions, and between sub-regions, will be adjusted by the census.

Japan: A blooming tree (left) in the mid of November 2008, near an artesian fountain in the central park from the Inzai (Chiba) campus of Tokyo Denki University, at sunset.

38. Special credit card

SUN: The special credit card (SCC) is another important element of Dediu Method.

EARTH: Yes, the special credit card (SCC) will be used to buy everything, to identify for voting, for census, for travel, for medical assistance, etc. The current private credit cards will continue to work as usual. The changes of the delimitations between regions, and also sub-regions, will be inputted on these cards, and no other work is needed.

Now a report writes that already there is a new end-to-end platform, that would enable governments to issue a biometric smart card to verify that the holder is virus free or has immunity. The issued smart card can be securely linked to a country's medical database and includes up-to-date encrypted data on the holder's COVID-19 profile.

Canada, Niagara Falls: the American Falls (21-30 m drop, 290 m wide), the Bridal Veil Falls (center-right, 21m) after Luna Island.

DM39. Viruses, microbes, bad bacteria

SUN: Who are the enemies of the people on Earth, according to Dediu Method?

EARTH: The enemies of the people on Earth are not other people, but viruses, microbes, bad bacteria and hundreds of deadly illnesses – all people on Earth will work together against these real enemies for all of us.

France, Paris: La Seine, on Parisis boat, looking to the left bank: the hop on hop off Batobus Odeon, Quai Anatole France, and Port de Solférino.

DM40. Non-violence

SUN: Benjamin Franklin (over 240 years ago) again gives good advice…...

EARTH: "Remember not only to say the right thing in the right place, but far more difficult still, to leave unsaid the wrong thing at the tempting moment." This is the precise recipe for a harmonious world.

SUN: Edison, over 90 years ago, is also famous for his insistence on peace….

EARTH: Yes, "Non-violence leads to the highest ethics, which is the goal of all evolution".

SUN: How do you establish non-violence, using Dediu Method?

EARTH: Non-violence is a strict requirement for all activities on Earth. The first rule for everybody on Earth comes from the Hippocratic Oath: Primum non nocere - first do not harm.

SUN: How will the doctors help?

EARTH: Medical doctors and assistants will make regular home visits to all people, to keep them healthy, and to prevent illnesses.

DM41. Truth

SUN: What about the truth in the world?

EARTH: Johann Wolfgang von Goethe reminded everybody that "Wisdom is found only in truth", therefore everything in the world must be based on truth, even if, sometimes, it is inconvenient for some.

SUN: Aeschylus (over 2,480 years ago) is so inspiring…..

EARTH: Yes, "In war, truth is the first casualty". These days it is really difficult to find the truth anytime.

SUN: Marcus Aurelius also ads a clear advice, over 1,841 years ago…

EARTH: "If it is not right, do not do it; if it is not true, do not say it."

SUN: Rousseau (over 250 years ago) is magnificent…..

EARTH: Yes, "Falsehood has an infinity of combinations, but truth has only one mode of being". For this we have plenty of misinformation, and the truth is very hard to find. This will certainly change, because we do need only truth in order to create a long term peaceful and harmonious society. Kant (over 220 years ago) also must be mentioned: "By a lie, a man… annihilates his dignity as a man". "Ingratitude is the essence of vileness".

SUN: Stendhal (over 180 years ago) is allegoric…..

EARTH: Yes, "The shepherd always tries to persuade the sheep that their interests, and his own, are the same". Well, many try this trick, but it does not work.

SUN: Truth is a big problem – how do you apply Dediu Method?

EARTH: People need only truth in order to create a long term peaceful and harmonious society.

SUN: And if someone lies?

EARTH: If someone lies – medical treatment will follow.

SUN: Remember Churchill (over 60 years ago) ….

EARTH: Yes, "A lie gets halfway around the world before the truth has a chance to get its pants on". So true these days.

France, Paris: La Seine, on Parisis boat, looking downriver: the south part of Pont des Invalides (1855, 152 m by 18 m), la Tour Eiffel (1889, 324 m, 279 m at the 3rd level observatory), and a passing boat (left).

DM42. Fundamental requirement

SUN: Tacitus, over 1,900 years ago, explains clearly…

EARTH: "A desire to resist oppression is implanted in the nature of man."

SUN: This wondrous Rousseau (over 250 years ago)….

EARTH: Yes, "Man was born free, and he is everywhere in chains." Now these chains are a little different in separate locations, but the chains of war, conflicts, forced military service, insufficient freedom, inadequate health service, broken education, and many others, are still with us, and the people are determined to eliminate them all.

SUN: What about freedom, using Dediu Method?

EARTH: Yes, freedom is a fundamental requirement on Earth.

SUN: Does freedom mean that everybody does what they want?

EARTH: No, it is well understood that this freedom refers to doing good things in a civilized manner, not for war, violence or similar bad things, which are against the wellbeing of the people.
Freedom goes hand in hand with responsibility.
People can assemble peacefully only.

SUN: The renowned Jefferson, over 200 years ago …..

EARTH: Yes, "All tyranny needs to gain a foothold is for people of good conscience to remain silent". Very clear and simple.
Also, Leonardo da Vinci (over 510 years ago): "Nothing strengthens authority so much as silence."

DM43. Economy

SUN: Economy – how will it be, according to Dediu Method?

EARTH: For economy it is clear that the free market economy, while not perfect, gives the best results, but all people will have the option to choose between friendly private services, and friendly government services. Independent assistants and monitors will make sure that there are no abuses. Sine qua non requirements for happiness are morality and free market.

SUN: And religion?

EARTH: The religion will be free, and is expected not to interfere with activities of the Advisors, and actually should help people.

SUN: Can you petition the Government?

EARTH: People of course can petition the small Word Government, and can change it anytime, if it does not perform as expected.

DM44. Budget surplus

SUN: Budget deficits are common for governments – how do you apply Dediu Method?

EARTH: All budgets will have a surplus of 2% - there will be a strict application of the Latin aphorism: "Sumptus censum ne superset" (Let not your spending exceed your income).

SUN: The great Horatius (over 2,030 years ago).....

EARTH: Yes, "Facile largire de alieno" (It is easy to be generous with things of another person). Unfortunately, this is officially done daily, but the people will soon change this. Here comes Reagan (over 20 years ago): "No government ever voluntarily reduces itself in size. Government programs, once launched, never disappear. Actually, a government bureau is the nearest thing to eternal life we'll ever see on this earth!" But the new World Government will voluntarily reduce itself in size.

Italy, Rome (753 BC): Fontana dei Quattro Fiumi (Fountain of the Four Rivers) by Gian Lorenzo Bernini, in 1651, in Piazza Navona.

DM45. Correcting errors

SUN: There are plenty of errors everywhere – what you do about this?

EARTH: Correcting errors is a permanent duty for everybody - Darwin (circa 140 years ago, around 1880) said "To kill an error is as good a service as, and sometimes even better than, the establishing of a new truth or fact."

SUN: Do you know another related aphorism?

EARTH: But of course! "Achievement is not permanent success, but how fast you recover from a fiasco." There will always be errors and fiascos, important is to quickly recover and to keep running.

Japan: Photographs and computer presentations at the High Energy Accelerator Research Organization (KEK, 1997) in Tsukuba Science City (1962), in Ibaraki, 60 km north-east of Tokyo.

DM46. Kindness

SUN: Well, kindness is really good, right?

EARTH: Kindness is a requirement for everybody.
Seneca (circa 1,960 years ago) said "Wherever there is a human being, there is an opportunity for a kindness."
This is a fundamental idea which must be constantly applied.

SUN: Sophocles (over 2,430 years ago) does good deeds…..

EARTH: Yes, "To be doing good deeds is man's most glorious task." And this is what all of us will be doing very soon.

France, Paris: La Seine, on Parisis boat, looking downriver: the center of Pont Alexandre III (1896-1900, for Tsar Alexandre III, the most ornate, with the sculpture Nymphs of the Seine and Art Nouveau lamps.

DM47. Highly mobile

SUN: Governments are usually fix in their old massive buildings –
how will this change using Dediu Method?

EARTH: All levels of government will be highly mobile - changing
of the capitals for the 10 regions, and for the 100 sub-regions, etc.
It is necessary to move the government close to the people, to be
able to quickly solve the local problems.
Locally the people will decide how to better organize themselves, to
be more efficient and harmonious, with the help of the world
government when necessary. Like in any big family, there will be
differences in organization and management, based on their abilities
and objectives, but all must be peaceful and harmonious. Conflicts
will be promptly resolved by the medical personnel, police, and
other assistants.

Canada, Niagara Falls: the American Falls (21-30 m drop, 290 m
wide, left), and the Horseshoe Falls (in Canada, 53 m drop, 790 m
wide, right), with a boat with tourists and an amazing rainbow.

DM48. World Police and Assistance

SUN: The Police Department is always necessary – what changes will you have?

EARTH: The United Nations will change in 2-3 years (for example, by 2024) into World Police and Assistance Organization (WPAO), to help local police in case of big natural disasters or big accidents, and will report to the top 10 Advisers. WPAO will be located in all capitals, and help the locals. When an emergency appears, they will quickly move to solve the emergency.

The police powers will be limited, and they will know and be friend with all the people in their jurisdiction – this is the key element of a civilized and peaceful Earth. If they notice a person with bad intentions, they immediately retain that person and call for a medical assistant (and other assistants, if necessary), to analyze and solve the issue very quickly.

Police will be people's friends everywhere, and they will always help people.

Japan: Mount Fuji (3,776 m, 1707 last eruption) seen from Kawaguchi city (left), near Kawaguchiko (Lake Kawaguchi, 6 km^2, 830 m elevation, right), 100 km south-west of Tokyo.

DM49. Prevention

SUN: Prevention of bad events is really difficult – what is your approach?

EARTH: Prevention of bad events is the main objective of everybody. If a bad event occurs, the police and their assistants will eliminate the consequences, reestablish the normal situation, and determine why the bad event occurred, in order to improve their activity, and prevent such bad events in the future.

Private property cannot be taken for public use, without just compensation, decided by at least 5 assistants.

A person cannot be deprived by government of life, liberty, or property, without having several doctors and other assistants agree: for life – at least 12; for liberty – at least 6; for property – at least 3.

A person cannot deprive another person of life, liberty, or property, which, unfortunately, occurs very frequently in the world, and very much effort and energy will be allocated to prevent such bad events.

In order to prevent bad things, the police, doctors and their assistants will be in permanent contact with all the people, by visiting them, phone calls, e-mails, tele-videos, and mail, to keep everybody calm and happy.

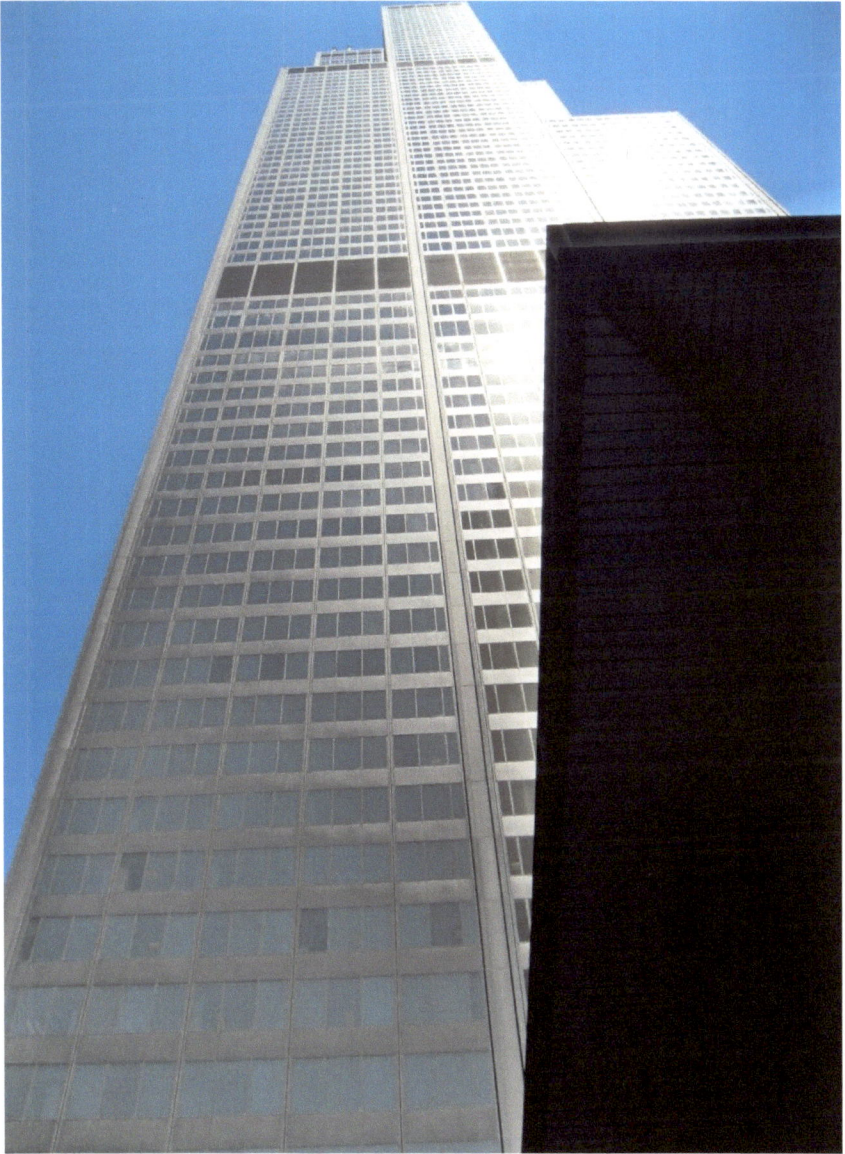

USA, Chicago 1837: Willis Tower (1973, 108 floors, 527 m), the tallest building in the USA, on South Franklin Street, near West Adams Street.

DM50. Non-stop working

SUN: You know, about 66% of the people of the world are working at any moment.

EARTH: Yes, therefore, non-stop working of all world government departments – especially medical, police, emergency, volunteers – will be carefully organized.

Paris, Île de la Cité, Pont au Change (1860): La Conciergerie (Palace of French Kings (950 – 1358), on Quai de l'Horloge), Pont Neuf (1578-1607, right, at the west corner of l'Île de la Cité).

DM51. Privacy

SUN: Privacy of discussions is a necessity.

EARTH: Indeed, in order to have serious and constructive discussions and negotiations, they must be private. Privacy and discipline are necessary for good government work. The results will be public and preserved, but not the private discussions.

Japan: In Shinjuku, view from the 45th fl., 202 m, of Tokyo Metropolitan Government Building: Tokyo Opera City Tower (234 m, 54 fl, 1996, center-left), Shinjuku Mitsui Building (224 m, 55 fl, 1974, center-right), Shinjuku Center Building (223 m, 54 fl, 1979, right).

DM52. Politeness

SUN: Politeness is so beautiful.

EARTH: Of course, and it is a strict requirement for the top management, and for all others, to be highly civilized, polite, courteous, harmonious and efficient. Who wants to work for the world government must have good manners. Harmony in the world starts from the harmony and good manners of the people in the world government.

SUN: Plato (over 2,370 years ago) has again a fine aphorism….

EARTH: Yes, "To prefer evil to good is not in the human nature; and when a man is compelled to choose one of two evils, no one will choose the greater when he might have the less." This is the foundation for people's request for long term peace and harmony.

Canada, Niagara Falls: Niagara SkyWheel in Dinosaur Park and Miniature Golf, near Clifton Hill and Oneida Lane, 1.5 km north of the Horseshoe Falls.

DM53. No conflicts

SUN: Volens, nolens, conflicts frequently appear.

EARTH: True – however, all conflicts must not only be quickly resolved, but they must be transformed in friendships. This is very important for long term stability. The medical personnel and others will work diligently to make sure that disputes are resolved, and then a friendship is developed. Only in this way the situation will become stable. People want peace, freedom, health, friendship and prosperity, therefore conflicts should be quickly resolved, and then the corrective medical treatment will include the transformation of hostility and aggressiveness into harmony and friendship.

SUN: We are so proud of Cicero (over 2,070 years ago)….

EARTH: Yes, "Friendship improves happiness and abates misery, by the doubling of our joy, and the dividing of our grief." For this all people want more friendship, and the medical personnel will help very much in this direction. Cicero also said: "A room without books is like a body without a soul."

DM54. Easy communication

SUN: Easy communication between all people is a high priority.

EARTH: Certainly, as a single big, over 7.7 B family on Earth, all people must be able to communicate easily with each other. For this reason, a common language and alphabet on Earth are needed. Because English is a de facto common language now, it will be taken as the basis of the world language, let's call it Mundo, which will be taught in all schools, and used in the world government. All the other languages will continue as secondary languages. The same is true for the Latin alphabet, which will be used everywhere, with other alphabets as secondary. The teachers will have a very significant role in implementing this.

Japan: Kawaguchi, near Kawaguchiko (Lake Kawaguchi, 6 km^2, 830 m elevation), 100 km south-west of Tokyo, with bonsai trees.

DM55. Global wealth

SUN: Global wealth is not too bad.

EARTH: Indeed, the 2018 Global Wealth Report from Credit Suisse shows that the total global wealth has reached $317 trillions (circa $41,000/person), which is encouraging, and all this wealth must be used only for peace.

Like in any big family, there are differences, because some work more, some spend less, some move faster, and, especially, some are sick – this is the main reason for differences: not all people can be equally sick, some people are sicker than others. However, all the people and the government will work to help each other.

It is a major responsibility of the Government to increase the global wealth, and to train those in need, to have better working abilities and opportunities.

SUN: Descartes (circa 380 years ago) helps everybody…..

EARTH: "It is not enough to have a good mind. The main thing is to use it well." This is the essence of sustainable peace and freedom for a long time.

Japan: Shinjuku is a ward of Tokyo, with many very tall buildings.

DM56. No bureaucracy

SUN: Bureaucracy is always a big issue.

EARTH: And the response is no bureaucracy – this is required by all people, and every day attention will be given for improvements in this direction. In a well-organized country, with all people working together in harmony, this can be accomplished in several years.

SUN: Rousseau (over 250 years ago) is so delightful….

EARTH: Yes, "No man has any natural authority over his fellow men." Some still ignore this obvious fact, but people will definitely correct this abnormal situation. We should add here "Arrogance and self-importance are everywhere, modesty is a rara avis (rare bird)".

Canada, Niagara Falls: Niagara River on the west end of the Horseshoe Falls (in Canada, 53 m drop, 790 m wide).

DM57. No duplication

SUN: Corruption and duplication also need attention.

EARTH: Sure, everybody will work really hard to completely eliminate corruption, organized crime and drug trafficking. Constant attention will be focused on avoiding duplication at all levels of the world government – there must be continuous collaboration between all levels, to prevent duplication, and to eliminate it, if it was found.

Italy, Rome (753 BC): a lemon tree in the front yard of an apartment close to Via Aurelia (started in 241 BC by C. Aurelius Cotta) and Via Graziano, about 2 km west of the Basilica San Pietro (1506 - 1626) and 4.5 km north-west from Colosseum (70).

DM58. Reserves and savings

SUN: Good reserves and savings are welcome.

EARTH: Certainly, each government department will have some reserves for special situations (natural disasters, big accidents), and the banks will also have good financial reserves. All people will be encouraged to save some money in banks with 5% interest.

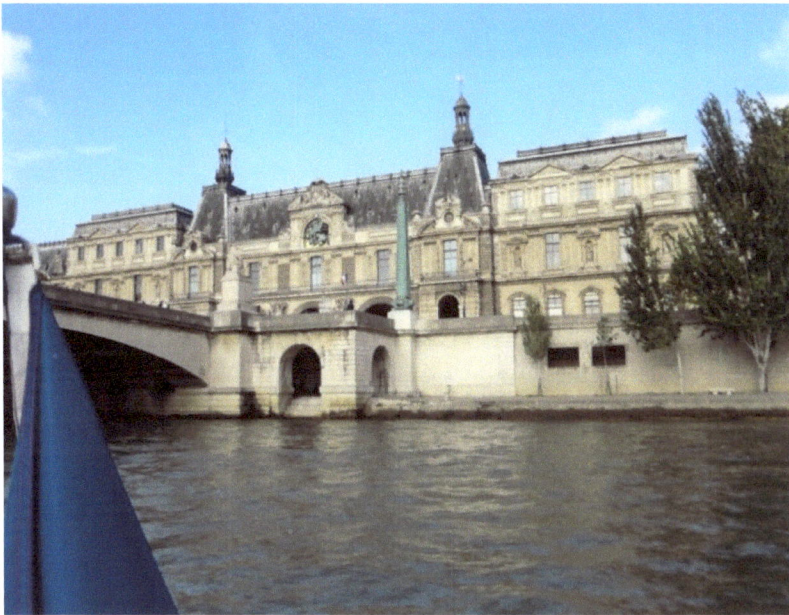

La Seine, on Parisis boat, looking to the right bank: the north end of Pont du Carrousel (1831-1834, left), the entrance to the Place du Carrousel (part of Musée du Louvre (1793)).

DM59. Integrity and efficiency

SUN: Integrity and efficiency can always be a little better.

EARTH: Right, inspectors will help the Government with the integrity and efficiency issues – always there are ways to improve the work. Inspectors will give advice regarding integrity and efficiency, and will take corrective actions when necessary.

Japan: In Shinjuku, from the 45th fl., 202 m, of Tokyo Metropoli. Gov Bg: Shinjuku Mitsui Bg (224 m, 55 fl, 1974, left), Sompo Japan Bldg. (193 m, 43 fl, 1976, center-left), Shinjuku Center Bldg. (223 m, 54 fl, 1979, center-left), Mode Gakuen Cocoon Tower (204 m, 50 fl, 2008, center-up), Keio Plaza Hotel (180 m, 47 fl, 1971, center).

DM60. Family assistance

SUN: First thing first: family assistance.

EARTH: No question about this. Because all families need assistance from time to time, and the big 7.7 B family on Earth contains billions of small families, all of them will have the assistance they need – this will be the result of one country well organized and managed.

Japan: the northern side of Kawaguchiko (Lake Kawaguchi, 6 km^2, 830 m elevation), with a splendid statue (left), 17 km north of Mt. Fuji (3,776 m, 1707 last eruption), 100 km south-west of Tokyo.

DM61. Harmony

SUN: Harmony can be achieved.

EARTH: Sure - because all people on Earth want to live in harmony right now, it will be relatively easy to implement this in one good and civilized country. This may include having small, beautiful and commonly agreed fences around properties, because good fences make good neighbors, and also helps with more privacy.

SUN: For harmony it is better to remember Churchill, who, about 60 years ago, explains…

EARTH: "Courage is what it takes to stand up and speak; courage is also what it takes to sit down and listen."

France, the south-east up corner of L'Opéra de Paris (1875): Poesie, Lyrique, Sculpture, Peinture, busts of composers Fromental Halévy (1799 – 1862, right) and Giacomo Meyerbeer (1794 – 1864, left).

DM62. Dispute resolution

SUN: Volens nolens disputes appear, and dispute resolution is required.

EARTH: Of course, and dispute resolution is not only Government's obligation, but it will be everybody's duty. There will be professional assistance from medical personnel, police, people assistance specialists, volunteers, religious organizations, and many others, but the bottom line is that everybody must avoid disputes.

When there are different opinions, just stay calm, express your opinion, listen to others, and continue calm the discussion until a compromise is reached. There is no need to spend much time and energy – let the people decide, and even if your idea is not temporarily accepted, there are chances that in the future you'll have more people agree with you.

Italy, Rome (753 BC): detail of the Altare della Patria (1925), with a view of Piazza Venezia, 150 m west from Trajan's Column (113)

DM63. No abuses

SUN: Plato (over 2,370 years ago), as usual, has excellent ideas…..

EARTH: "The measure of a man is what he does with power." And many with power, unfortunately, disappoint us badly.

SUN: Well, power creates conditions for abuses, which must be corrected.

EARTH: Indeed, special attention will be given by Advisors to avoid abuses and wrong interpretations of the rules. All assistants (doctors, mathematicians, CEOs, engineers and teachers) will closely monitor all activities, to avoid abuses and wrong interpretations of the rules. This requirement of not having abuses is demanding – but this is a general job, not only for Government, but for everybody, as part of the big family, we just don't need abuses.

   The abuse, in some places, of confiscating the land by some government bureaucrats, will be eliminated – the land belongs to the people, not the government.

   The abuse, in some places, of having trains, airplanes, and others making unhealthy noises, with the government support, will be eliminated – peoples' health has always priority.

   The abuse, in some places, of having to change the clocks twice a year will be eliminated – only the normal local time zones will be used.

   If abuses are observed, they will be immediately reported to the Government, and corrected, in general, by the People Assistance Department, which will have personnel, including medical assistants, to analyze and promptly solve the abuses.

France, Paris: La Seine, on Parisis boat, looking upstream to the left bank: Port de Suffren with Vedettes de Paris Croisières (Cruises), near Quai Branly, the north-west and south-west sides of la Tour Eiffel (1889, 324 m, 279 m at the 3rd level observatory), with pilier nord on the left, pilier est on the center left back, pilier vest on the center front, and pilier sud on the right.

DM64. Free commerce

SUN: So beautiful – free commerce, speech, press!

EARTH: True - in one country, with one market, the commerce between the people on Earth will be free of taxes, tariffs, duties, etc. – plenty of opportunities for everybody.

The speech will be free and responsible. It is expected not to call for war, violence, or similar destructive activities. People want peace, freedom, health, friendship and prosperity.

The press will be free and responsible. It is expected not to call for war, violence, or similar destructive activities. People want peace, freedom, health, friendship and prosperity.

People can assemble peacefully only, with police for help. It is expected not to call for war, violence, or similar destructive activities. People want peace, freedom, health, friendship and prosperity.

Japan, Kyoto (678): the Nishi Hongan-ji Temple ("Western Temple of the Original Vow", 1602, on the west side of Horikawa Dori), with people dressed in white attending a religious ceremony.

DM65. Plenty of jobs

SUN: Will you have enough jobs?

EARTH: Yes, there will always be plenty of jobs at world minimum wage (assisting other people, for example), and the standard situation will be this: more jobs than available people, so people will choose the jobs they like the most.

No unemployment, no homelessness, no begging, no tipping – just all working harmoniously, having good houses, and helping each other.

Chicago, 1837: a beautiful interior path between nice buildings on the south side of the West Belmont Ave, between North Hudson Ave on the east (left) and N. Pine Grove Ave on the west (right).

DM66. Limited number of rules

SUN: Tacitus said something, over 1,900 years ago…

EARTH: Corruptissima re publica plurimae leges (In a very corrupt state are the most laws).

SUN: And, above all, remember Edison, over 90 years ago, for some small projects…

EARTH: "Hell, there are no rules here - we're trying to accomplish something."

SUN: However, Sophocles, over 2,430 years ago, reminds us of the need for rules…

EARTH: "There is no greater evil than anarchy."

SUN: The more rules, the less respect for them.

EARTH: It is well known – therefore all rules proposed by Advisers must be approved by their 5 assistants (doctors, mathematicians, CEOs, engineers and teachers), and for any new rule over 2,000 basic rules (each rule on at most half a page, total 1,000 pages), at least on old rule must be eliminated.

All the rules can be changed or eliminated when a majority of the people or their Advisors agree, but some fundamental peace and order rules will remain.

DM67. Improvements

SUN: When the Constitution of the World can be changed?

EARTH: The Constitution of the World can be improved when 66% of the voters agree.

France: La Seine, on Parisis boat, looking upriver: the center of Pont Alexandre III (1896-1900, with the sculpture Nymphs of the Neva and Art Nouveau lamps).

DM68. Purpose

SUN: Therefore, what is the purpose for all people on Earth?

EARTH: The purpose for all people on Earth is to be healthy, to live in peace, freedom and harmony, to be prosperous, and to prepare to expand to the Moon, asteroids, Mars, and other places in the Universe, which can support life.

Japan, Kyoto (678): the gate to Shinshu Honbyo Temple (1321, called until 1987 Higashi Hongan-Ji) on the west side of Karasuma Dori, north of Shichijo Dori and south of Hanayacho Dori.

DM69. Immediate objectives

SUN: Do you have immediate objectives for everybody?

EARTH: Important immediate objectives for everybody are:
- Reserve time for happiness.
- Use robots and automated processes, work less, and spend more time with your family.
- The weekend will be like a small vacation.
- Prevent burnout.
- Make civilized behavior and harmony everywhere an important issue.
- Eliminate stress.
- Help friends and colleagues.
- Keep everybody relaxed, calm, friendly, patient, and happy.

SUN: Pliny the Younger, about 1,910 years ago, had a good observation.

EARTH: Yes: "However often you may have done them a favor, if you once refuse, they forget everything except your refusal." Therefore, it is important to remind this aphorism to those who are upset by a refusal, after many favors.

SUN: And be patient, as Cato the Elder, about 2,170 years ago, said.

EARTH: "Patience is the greatest of all virtues."

Japan: In Shinjuku, Shinjuku Center Building (223 m, 54 fl, 1979, left), Mode Gakuen Cocoon Tower (204 m, 50 fl, 2008, center-left), Keio Plaza Hotel North Tower (180 m, 47 fl, 1971, center-right).

DM70. Starting this new structure

SUN: Any idea how to start this new structure of the world?

EARTH: To start this new structure of the world, one idea could be this: the first Honorific World Observer (from UN, for example) could invite 10 Presidents form big countries (like USA, China, Russia, UK, India, France, Japan, Germany, Brasil, and Egypt) to be the first 10 Advisors Level 4, starting, for example, on January 1st, 2021, for 10 months, until November 1st, 2021, when the new calm and noiseless elections will take place. The same for the 100 Advisers Level 3, and so on.

SUN: Listen again to Plato (over 2,370 years ago)….

EARTH: Yes, with great pleasure: "Those who intend on becoming great should love neither themselves nor their own things, but only what is just, whether it happens to be done by themselves or others." Oh, well, we are still very far from this necessary situation.

La Seine, on Parisis boat, looking upriver to south-east: on the left bank, Port des Saints-Pères, Quai de Conti, l'Institute de France (1795, (the north-west Pavilion (right), the Cupola (center) and the south-east Pavilion (left)), grouping five Académies, including l'Académie française (1635) and l'Académie des sciences (1666)).

DM71. Where the Constitution of the World is in force

SUN: And where the Constitution of the World is in force?

EARTH: The Constitution of the World is in force not only on Earth, but also in the space around Earth, on the Moon, Mars, asteroids and any other places were the very good people on Earth will be moving in the future.

Japan, Kyoto, 678 (it was the imperial capital of Japan for over 1,000 years): 2 rainbows (center and center-right, over Hitachi) on the east part of Kyoto.

DM72. When? We cannot wait!

SUN: Any time limitations?

EARTH: The Constitution of the World is intended for at least 10,000 years of harmonious living on the happy Earth.

    The Constitution of the World is ready to come into force, and to be put into practice, for the benefit of all people on Earth, on 6 March 2020, and it is ready to remain into force, and enjoyed by all people at least until 6 March 12020.

USA: Chicago, 1837: a good-looking ornament over the entrance to the building at 457 and 459 West Belmont Ave.

Bibliography

"The Histories" by Polybius
"Discours de la Méthode" by René Descartes
"Meditationes de prima philosophia" by René Descartes
"Philosophiae Naturalis Principia Mathematica" by Isaac Newton
Chinese encyclopedia Gujin Tushu Jicheng (Imperial Encyclopedia)
"Encyclopédie" by Jean-Baptiste le Rond d'Alembert and Denis Diderot
"Encyclopaedia Britannica" by over 4,400 contributors
"Encyclopedia Americana" by Francis Lieber
Other sources include: UPI, CNBC, AP, Nasdaq, Reuters, EDGAR, AFP, Recode, Europa Press, Bloomberg News, Fox News, USA, Deutsche Presse-Agentur, MSNBC, BBC, Australian Associated Press, Agência Brasil, The Canadian Press (La Presse Canadienne), Middle East News Agency, Baltic News Service, Suomen Tietotoimisto, Athens-Macedonian News Agency, Asian News International, Inter Press Service, Kyodo News, Notimex, Algemeen Nederlands Persbureau, AGERPRES, Newsis, Tidningarnas Telegrambyrå, Swiss Telegraphic Agency, Central News Agency, ANKA news agency, Agenzia Fides

Michael M. Dediu is also the author of these books (which can be found on Amazon.com, and www.derc.com):

1. Aphorisms and quotations – with examples and explanations
2. Axioms, aphorisms and quotations – with examples and explanations
3. 100 Great Personalities and their Quotations
4. Professor Petre P. Teodorescu – A Great Mathematician and Engineer
5. Professor Ioan Goia – A Dedicated Engineering Professor
6. Venice (Venezia) – a new perspective. A short presentation with photographs
7. La Serenissima (Venice) - a new photographic perspective. A short presentation with many photos

USA, Chicago, 1837: John Hancock Center (1969, 100 fl, 457 m), at 875 North Michigan Avenue.

8. Grand Canal – Venice. A new photographic viewpoint. A short presentation with many photos

9. Piazza San Marco – Venice. A different photographic view. A short presentation with many photos

10. Roma (Rome) - La Città Eterna. A new photographic view. A short presentation with many photos

11. Why is Rome so Fascinating? A short presentation with many photos

12. Rome, Boston and Helsinki. A short photographic presentation

13. Rome and Tokyo – two captivating cities. A short photographic presentation

14. Beautiful Places on Earth – A new photographic presentation

15. From Niagara Falls to Mount Fuji via Rome - A novel photographic presentation

16. From the USA and Canada to Italy and Japan - A fresh photographic presentation

17. Paris – Why So Many Call This City Mon Amour - A lovely photographic presentation

18. The City of Light – Paris (La Ville-Lumière) - A kaleidoscopic photographic presentation

19. Paris (Lutetia Parisiorum) – the romance capital of the world - A kaleidoscopic photographic view

20. Paris and Tokyo – a joyful photographic presentation. With a preamble about the Universe

21. From USA to Japan via Canada – A cheerful photographic documentary

22. 200 Wonderful Places, In The Last 50 Years – A personal photographic documentary

23. Must see places in USA and Japan - A kaleidoscopic photographic documentary

24. Grandeurs of the World - A kaleidoscopic photographic documentary

25. Corneliu Leu – writer on the same wavelength as Mark Twain. An American viewpoint

26. From Berkeley to Pompeii via Rome – A kaleidoscopic photographic documentary

27. From America to Europe via Japan - A kaleidoscopic photographic documentary

28. Discover America and Japan - A photographic documentary

29. J. R. Lucas – philosopher on a creative parallel with Plato, An American viewpoint

30. From America to Switzerland via France - A photographic documentary

31. From Bretton Woods to New York via Cape Cod - A photographic documentary

32. Splendid Places on the Atlantic Coast of the U. S. A. - A photographic documentary

33. Fourteen nice Cities on three Continents - A photographic documentary

34. 17 Picturesque Cities on the World Map - A photographic documentary

35. Unforgettable Places from Four Continents, including Trump buildings - A photographic documentary

36. Dediu Newsletter, Volume 1, Number 1, 6 December 2016 – Monthly news, review, comments and suggestions for a better and wiser world

37. Dediu Newsletter, Volume 1, Number 2, 6 January 2017 (available also at www.derc.com).

38. Dediu Newsletter, Volume 1, Number 3, 6 February 2017 (available at www.derc.com).

39. London and Greenwich, - A photographic documentary

40. Dediu Newsletter, Volume 1, Number 4, 6 March 2017 (available also at www.derc.com).

41. Dediu Newsletter, Volume 1, Number 5, 6 April 2017 (available also at www.derc.com).

42. Dediu Newsletter, Volume 1, Number 6, 6 May 2017 (available also at www.derc.com).

43. Dediu Newsletter, Volume 1, Number 7, 6 June 2017 (available also at www.derc.com).

44. London, Oxford and Cambridge, A photographic documentary

45. Dediu Newsletter, Volume 1, Number 8, 6 July 2017 (available also at www.derc.com).

46. Dediu Newsletter, Volume 1, Number 9, 6 August 2017 (available also at www.derc.com).

47. Dediu Newsletter, Volume 1, Number 10, 6 September 2017 (available also at www.derc.com).

Italy, Roma: Fontana di Trevi (1732 – 1762). Standing 26.3 m high and 49.15 m wide, it is located on Palazzo di Poli (1566). Tritons guide Oceanus' shell chariot, calming hippocampi. In the center an imaginatively modeled triumphal arch is placed over on the palazzo façade. The center niche, or exedra, framing Oceanus, has free-standing columns for greatest light and shade. Pietro Bracci's Oceanus (god of all water) is the central sculpture.

48. Three Great Professors: President Woodrow Wilson, Historian German Arciniegas, and Mathematician Gheorghe Vranceanu – A chronological and photographic documentary

49. Dediu Newsletter, Volume 1, Number 11, 6 October 2017 (available also at www.derc.com).

50. Dediu Newsletter, Volume 1, Number 12, 6 November 2017 (available also at www.derc.com).

51. Dediu Newsletter, Volume 2, Number 1 (13), 6 December 2017 (available also at www.derc.com).

52. Two Great Leaders: Augustus and George Washington - A chronological and photographic documentary

53. Dediu Newsletter, Volume 2, Number 2 (14), 6 January 2018 (available also at www.derc.com).

54. Newton, Benjamin Franklin, and Gauss, A chronological and photographic documentary

55. Dediu Newsletter, Volume 2, Number 3 (15), 6 February 2018 (available also at www.derc.com).

56. 2017: World Top Events, But Many Little Known, A chronological and photographic documentary

57. Dediu Newsletter, Volume 2, Number 4 (16), 6 March 2018 (available also at www.derc.com).

58. Vergilius, Horatius, Ovidius, and Shakespeare - A chronological and photographic documentary.

59. Dediu Newsletter, Volume 2, Number 5 (17), 6 April 2018 (available also at www.derc.com).

60. Dediu Newsletter, Volume 2, Number 6 (18), 6 May 2018 (available also at www.derc.com).

61. Vivaldi, Bach, Mozart, and Verdi - A chronological and photographic documentary.

62. Dediu Newsletter, Volume 2, Number 7 (19), 6 June 2018 (available also at www.derc.com).

63. Dediu Newsletter, Volume 2, Number 8 (20), 6 July 2018 (available also at www.derc.com).

64. Dediu Newsletter, Volume 2, Number 9 (21), 6 August 2018 (available also at www.derc.com).

65. World History, a new perspective - A chronological and photographic documentary.

66. World Humor History with over 100 Jokes, a new perspective - A chronological and photographic documentary
67. Dediu Newsletter, Volume 2, Number 10 (22), 6 September 2018 (available also at www.derc.com).
68. Dediu Newsletter, Volume 2, Number 11 (23), 6 October 2018 (available also at www.derc.com).
69. Dediu Newsletter, Volume 2, Number 12 (24), 6 November 2018
70. Da Vinci, Michelangelo, Rembrandt, Rodin - A chronological and photographic documentary
71. Dediu Newsletter, Volume 3, Number 1 (25), 6 December 2018
72. Dediu Newsletter, Volume 3, Number 2 (26), 6 January 2019
73. From Euclid to Edison – revelries in the past 75 years - A chronological and photographic documentary
74. – Socrates to Churchill Aphorisms celebrated after 1960 - A chronological and photographic documentary
75. - Dediu Newsletter, Volume 3, Number 3 (27), 6 February 2019
76. – Hippocrates to Fleming: Medicine History celebrated after 1943 - A chronological and photographic documentary
77. - Dediu Newsletter, Volume 3, Number 4 (28), 6 March 2019
78. - Dediu Newsletter, Volume 3, Number 5 (29), 6 April 2019
79 – Archimedes to Ford: Invention History celebrated after 1943 - A chronological and photographic documentary
80 - Dediu Newsletter, Volume 3, Number 6 (30), 6 May 2019
81 – Sutherland to Pavarotti: Great Singers History - A chronological and photographic documentary
82 - Dediu Newsletter, Volume 3, Number 7 (31), 6 June 2019
83 - Dediu Newsletter, Volume 3, Number 8 (32), 6 July 2019
84 – Augustus to Rockefeller: History of the Wealthiest People - A chronological and photographic documentary
85 - Dediu Newsletter, Volume 3, Number 9 (33), 6 August 2019
86 – Pythagoras to Fermi: History of Science - A chronological and photographic documentary
87 - Dediu Newsletter, Volume 3, Number 10 (34), 6 September 2019
88 – Our Future is Sustainable Peace and Prosperity – Moving from conflicts to harmony and peace
89 - Dediu Newsletter, Volume 3, Number 11 (35), 6 October 2019 – World Monthly Report with news

90 – Our Future Depends on Good World Educations – Moving from frail education to solid education
91 - Dediu Newsletter, Volume 3, Number 12 (36), 6 November 2019 – World Monthly Report with News and Suggestions for Sustainable Peace, Freedom and Prosperity
92 – Friendly, Helpful & Smart World Management - Moving from bureaucracy to responsive world management
93 – If You Want Peace, Prepare for Peace! – Moving from preparation for war to preparation for peace
94 - Dediu Newsletter, Volume 4, Number 1 (37), 6 December 2019 – World Monthly Report with News and Suggestions for Sustainable Peace, Freedom and Prosperity
95 – World with One Country & its Ten Friendly Regions - Moving from 195 disagreeing countries, to 1 country with 10 collaborating regions
96 - Dediu Newsletter, Volume 4, Number 2 (38), 6 January 2020 – World Monthly Report with News and Suggestions for Sustainable Peace, Freedom and Prosperity
97 – After 10,000 Years of Conflicts, People want 10,000 Years of Harmony - Moving from continuous wars to stable peace
98 - Dediu Newsletter, Volume 4, Number 3 (39), 6 February 2020 – World Monthly Report with News and Suggestions for Sustainable Peace, Freedom and Prosperity
99 – The Constitution of the World – Moving from many unsustainable constitutions, to just one Constitution of the World
100 - Dediu Newsletter, Volume 4, Number 4 (40), 6 March 2020 – World Monthly Report with News and Suggestions for Sustainable Peace, Freedom and Prosperity
101 - Dediu Newsletter, Volume 4, Number 5 (41), 6 April 2020 – World Monthly Report
102 - Dediu Newsletter, Volume 4, Number 6 (42), 6 May 2020 – World Monthly Report
103 – World Constitution Implementation – Moving from violent changes, to smooth transition to the Constitution of the World
104 - Dediu Newsletter, Volume 4, Number 7 (43), 6 June 2020 – World Monthly Report
105 - Dediu Newsletter, Volume 4, Number 8 (44), 6 July 2020 – World Monthly Report

Italy, Venezia: In the middle of the west façade of the Basilica di San Marco, we see the central bronze-fashioned door, in a round-arched portal, encircled by polychrome marble columns. Above this door there are three round bas-relief cycles of Romanesque art. A Japanese couple, with their Japanese photographer, make their wedding photographs in this most beautiful place.

www.ingramcontent.com/pod-product-compliance
Lightning Source LLC
Chambersburg PA
CBHW041309210326
41599CB00003B/39